I0487423

SIX PACK

A REFRESHING COLLECTION OF UTILITIES FOR APPLE IIGS SYSTEM 6

by Bill Tudor

Quality Computers

Produced by:
Brian Wiser & Bill Martens

 Apple PugetSound Program Library Exchange

Six Pack

www.callapple.org

ISBN: 978-0-359-74615-6

ACKNOWLEDGEMENTS

Six Pack was programmed by Bill Tudor, with manual by Jerry Kindall, and originally published by Quality Computers, Inc. in 1992.

This new manual, produced in coordination with Quality Computers president Joe Gleason, is released with his permission and is copyright by A.P.P.L.E.. Our thanks to Joe Gleason for kindly providing the licensing to create this re-production and for his support during the process.

The Cover and Book were redesigned by Brian Wiser.

PRODUCTION

Brian Wiser → Design, Layout, Editing
Bill Martens → Scanning, Production, Disk Updates

DISCLAIMER

About Bill Tudor

Bill Tudor was a programmer who was quite prolific in the Apple II and IIGS arena, having published more than a dozen programs for the IIGS. In addition to writing *Six Pack* for Quality Computers, he wrote PFX, Get Set With ProDOS, and OmniType for *Nibble* magazine. Many of his utilities and plugins are still used today in the latest versions of GS/OS.

About the Producers

Brian Wiser

Brian Wiser is a long-time consultant, enthusiast and historian of Apple, the Apple II and Macintosh. Steve Wozniak and Steve Jobs, as well as *Creative Computing*, *Nibble, InCider,* and *A+* magazines were early influences.

Brian designed, edited, and co-produced many books including: *Nibble Viewpoints: Business Insights From The Computing Revolution*, *Cyber Jack: The Adventures of Robert Clardy and Synergistic Software*, *Synergistic Software: The Early Games*, *The Colossal Computer Cartoon Book: Enhanced Edition*, *What's Where in the Apple: Enhanced Edition,* and *The WOZPAK: Special Edition* – an important Apple II historical book with Steve Wozniak's restored original, technical handwritten notes.

He passionately preserves and archives all facets of Apple's history, and noteworthy related companies such as Beagle Bros and Applied Engineering, featured on AppleArchives.com. His writing, interviews and books are featured on the technology news site CallApple.org and in *Call-A.P.P.L.E.* magazine that he co-produces. Brian also co-produced the retro iOS game *Structris*.

In 2005, Brian was cast as an extra in Joss Whedon's movie *Serenity*, leading him to being a producer and director for the documentary film *Done The Impossible: The Fans' Tale of Firefly & Serenity*. He brought some of the *Firefly* cast aboard his Browncoat Cruise and recruited several of the *Firefly* cast to appear in a film for charity. Brian speaks about his adventures to large audiences at conventions around the country.

Bill Martens

Bill Martens is a systems engineer specializing in office infrastructures and has been programming since 1976. The DEC PDP 11/40 with ASR-33 Teletypes and CRT's were his first computing platforms with his first forays in the Apple world coming with the Apple II computer.

Influences in Bill's computing life came from *Byte* magazine, *Creative Computing* magazine, and *Call-A.P.P.L.E.* magazine as well as his mentors Samuel Perkins, Don Williams, Joff Morgan, and Mike Christensen.

Bill is a co-producer of many books including *What's Where in the Apple: Enhanced Edition, The WOZPAK: Special Edition, Nibble Viewpoints: Business Insights From The Computing Revolution*, and co-programmer for the iOS version of the retro game *Structris*. He has written many articles which have appeared in user group newsletters and magazines such as *Call-A.P.P.L.E.*.

Bill worked for Apple Pugetsound Program Library Exchange (A.P.P.L.E.) under Val Golding and Dick Hubert as a data manager and programmer in the 1980s, and is the current president of the A.P.P.L.E. user group established in 1978. He reorganized A.P.P.L.E. and restarted *Call-A.P.P.L.E.* magazine in 2002. He is the production editor for the A.P.P.L.E. website CallApple.org, writes science fiction novels in his spare time, and is a retired semi-pro football player.

Contents

Quality Computers

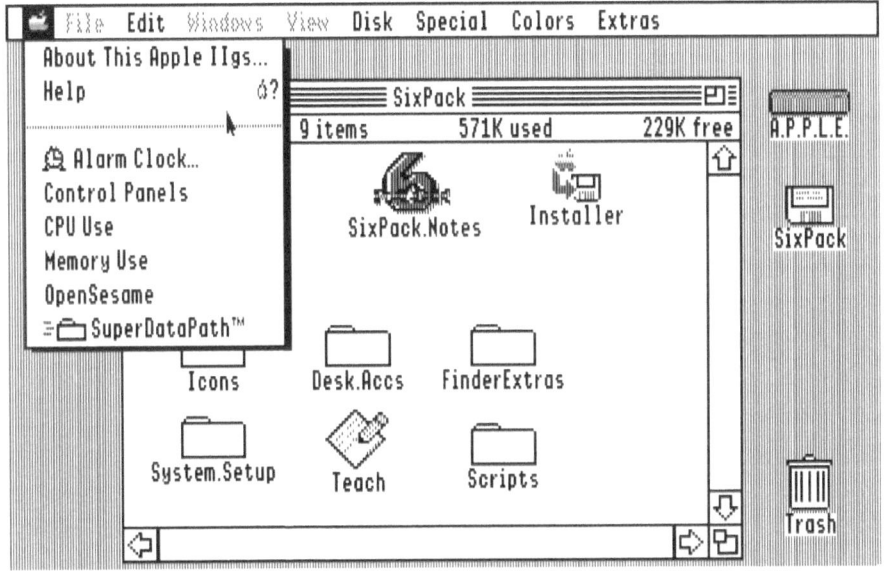

What is Six Pack?

Six Pack is a collection of fifteen accessory programs for Apple IIGS System 6. Most of these programs are Finder Extras, although a few are New Desk Accessories (NDAs). The programs are completely independent-you can install one, some, or all of them. (Some of them work with certain other programs in the system, but that's optional.)

Finder Extras & New Desk Accessories

A Finder Extra is a program that adds features to the System 6 Finder. The Finder is usually the first program you use when you start up your computer – it's the program that displays your disks and their contents and allows you to copy and rename files and launch application programs. Most Finder Extras add one or more menu items to the Finder's Extras menu. (If you've never seen the Extras menu, it's probably because you don't have any Finder Extras.)

A New Desk Accessory is a program that appears on your IIGS's Apple menu. New Desk Accessories (or NDAs) are available in any IIGS Desktop program – virtually any program that has a multicolored Apple in the menu bar – including, but not limited to, the Finder. The System 6 Control Panel is an NDA, as are the Puzzle and Calculator.

Six Pack Components

Six Pack includes 10 Finder Extras:

MoreInfo	PrintCatalog	FileCompare
HotKeys	Crypt	PrintCatalog
SelectIcons	FilePeeker	IR
CDEV Alias	WorkSet	

It also includes five New Desk Accessories (NDAs):

Alarm Clock	OpenSesame	SuperDataPath
CPU Use	Memory Use	

Six Pack Requirements

Six Pack requires Apple IIGS System Software 6.0, a hard drive, and at least two megabytes of RAM. (With the minimal two megabyte configuration, you may not be able to use all of *Six Pack's* functions at once, or you may have to do without some parts of System 6. We recommend at least three megabytes of RAM if you want to run a complete version of System 6 and all the *Six Pack* programs.)

What You Should Know

We assume you're familiar with basic Finder operations and how standard IIGS programs work. In particular, you need to know about:

- Selecting and opening icons in the Finder
- Selecting more than one icon by shift-clicking
- Differences between application, document, and folder icons

- Doing the usual things to icons (copy, move, delete, rename)
- How Dialogs, Standard File, Checkboxes, Radio Buttons, Line-edit Fields, Pull-down Menus, and Pop-up Menus work

If you're not familiar with these and other common IIGS features, we suggest a reference book like the one that came with your IIGS, Apple's System Software user manuals, or *The System 6 Book* from Quality Computers.

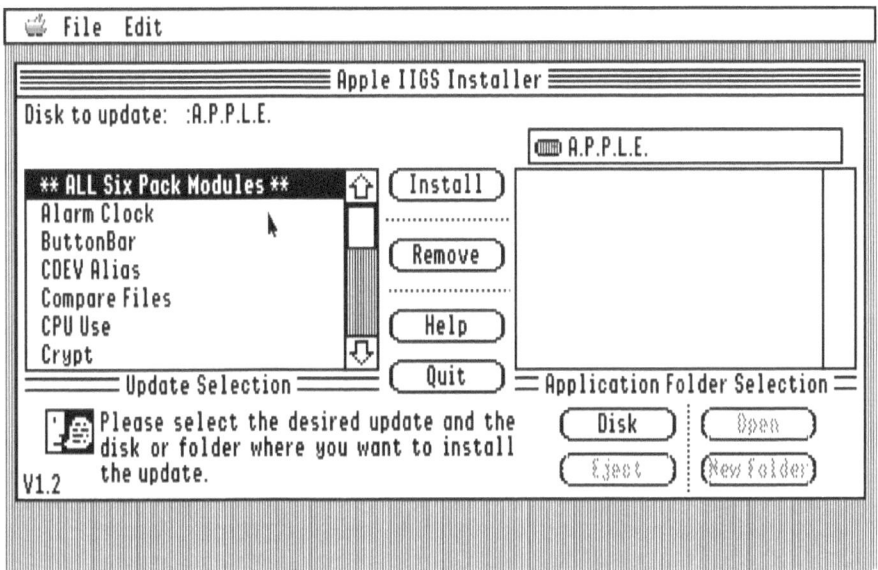

Getting Started

Before you install any components of *Six Pack*, you may want to skim through the rest of this manual and decide which programs you want to install. (The first paragraph of each section describes what the program described in that section does.) Or, if you have enough memory, you may want to install all of the *Six Pack* programs – you can always remove or disable the ones you don't use later.

Six Pack uses the standard Apple IIGS Installer to install its programs on your hard drive. If you installed System 6 yourself, you probably have used this program already. If your hard drive came with System 6 already installed, you may not be familiar with the Installer. Don't worry – it's simple. Here's how to do it:

1. Start up your IIGS from your hard drive, just as you usually do. Wait until the Finder appears.

    If you don't usually start up into the Finder, but instead use another program selector such as *Salvation Supreme*,

ProSel, or *Universe Master* – you'll need to launch the Finder from your usual program selector. Check your program selector's manual for information on how to do this. Don't continue until you're in the Finder.

2. When the Finder appears, insert the S*ix Pack* disk. The Finder will read the disk and display a window containing the Installer icon.

3. Double-click the Installer icon to launch the Installer.

4. The Installer screen will appear. There's a lot of stuff on the Installer screen, but for now you can ignore everything but the scrolling list on the left side of the screen. This list contains all the *Six Pack* components.

5. Select the programs you want to install. To select a single item, just click it. To select more than one item, click the first item normally, then hold down the ⌘ (Open Apple) key and click the additional items. (The ⌘ key tells the Installer to install the item you click in addition to the ones you've already selected. Clicking without the ⌘ key tells the Installer to install only the item you click.)

    For your convenience, there's also an All Modules item, which installs all of the *Six Pack* modules onto your hard drive. If you select that item, there's no need to select the individual modules listed below it.

6. Once you've selected the modules you want to install, click the "Install" button in the middle of the screen. The installation process will begin.

7. Click the Installer's "Quit" button. The Installer will tell you that you need to restart. Click the "Restart" button.

8. The *Six Pack* modules you requested are now installed and should be available when the Finder reappears. Congratulations!

Customizing Installation

When you install *Six Pack* on your hard drive, the Installer puts all the *Six Pack* NDAs into your System Folder in a folder called Desk. Accs. It puts all the Finder Extras into your System Folder in a folder called FinderExtras. (The exception is *IR* If you install *IR*, it is placed in the System.Setup folder.)

This installation means that NDAs will always be in memory once you've started your system (since they can be used in any IIGS program), but Finder Extras will only use memory when you're in the Finder (since only the Finder can use them). This gives you the maximum amount of free memory when you aren't in the Finder, but it means that the Finder has to reload the Extras from your hard drive whenever you quit a program, which can take several seconds.

If you have plenty of memory (four megabytes of RAM or more), you can move the Finder Extras from the FinderExtras folder to the System.Setup folder. (You can do this just by dragging the files from one window to another in the Finder.) If you do this, the Finder Extras will always be in memory, and returning to the Finder after running another program will be quite a bit faster. (If you want, you can keep some Finder Extras in FinderExtras and some in System. Setup.)

We've also included a Finder Extra called *IR* which allows you to load Finder Extras and NDAs after you've started up your computer. Install *IR* and move the other *Six Pack* files to some other folder. You'll then be able to install any of the *Six Pack* files by double-clicking them in the Finder. That way, you can start up with no *Six Pack* modules and install only the ones you need, when you need them. (See the section on *IR* in this manual for more information on this program.)

If you decide you don't want to use one of the *Six Pack* modules you've installed, there's no need to delete it. Instead, find the file you want to disable (in the FinderExtras, System.Setup, or Desk.Accs folders), click it once, choose "Get Info" from the File menu, click the "Inactive" checkbox, and close the Info window. Then restart your system. The IIGS completely ignores Finder Extras and NDAs you've disabled this way – they don't take up any memory and they don't slow down your startup. (Of course, you can also drag a module to the Trash to remove it permanently if you need the disk space.)

We also suggest taking a look at *Signature GS* from Quality Computers. Besides the screen blanker, desktop painter, and sound chooser, which are nifty all by themselves, there's also a Control Panel called Boot Master, which will allow you to activate and deactivate *Six Pack* modules from one master control panel and let you save "snapshots" of your configuration for later use.

Using the Modules

The rest of this manual is dedicated to the *Six Pack* modules themselves. There's a section for each module. Read the instructions in any order you like, but please do read them. Not only will you find the answers to questions you may have about using the programs, but you'll learn about features you might never have noticed if you hadn't read the manual.

Alarm Clock   **3**

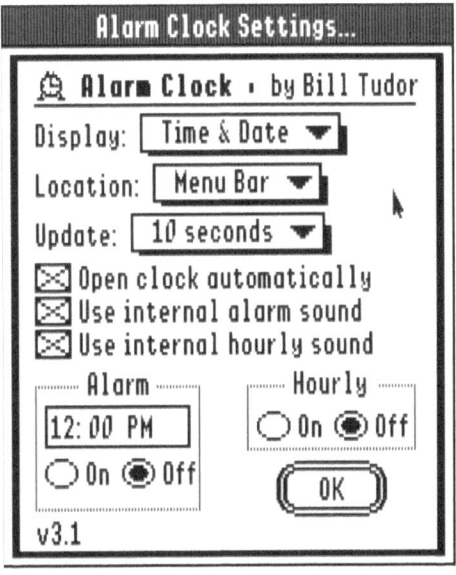

What It Does

The *Alarm Clock* displays the current date and time (or just the time) in the menu bar of IIGS programs, including the Finder, *AppleWorks GS*, *HyperStudio*, *Platinum Paint*, and dozens of other programs. The *Alarm Clock* also includes:

- Clock display in menu bar or in separate window
- Automatic opening of clock when a program is launched
- Adjustable alarm and optional hourly chime
- No interrupts or tool patches for maximum compatibility

How to Use It

When *Alarm Clock* is installed, you'll notice the time and date in the upper right hand corner of your screen (on the menu bar) or in a window. (If you don't see the time and date, make sure *Alarm Clock* is installed properly, restart, and check again.)

To adjust the clock settings, select *Alarm Clock* from the Apple menu. You can change the following settings:

Display   Select "Time & Date" or "Time Only" from the popup menu.

Location   Select "Menu Bar" or "Window" by choosing the appropriate option from this pop-up menu. (Some programs have long menu bars that don't leave room for the clock, or run in the 320-pixel graphics mode. The "Window" option is useful in these situations.)

Update   Choose how frequently to update the time display: once every ten seconds, once every five seconds, or every second. The update rate is approximate because *Alarm Clock* doesn't use interrupts. (Interrupts would allow more regular updating of the clock but could cause compatibility problems.) We suggest the 10 second update rate. You probably spend enough time waiting for your computer without making it update the clock every second.

Hourly   Turn the hourly chime (a beep on the hour) on and off with these two radio buttons.

Alarm   Turn the alarm on and off using the radio buttons. To set the alarm time, click on the hour, the minute, or the AM/PM symbol. Click the tiny arrows that appear to the right of the time to change the selected portion of the time. You can also use the Up and Down arrow keys or just type the desired time.

Open Clock   *Alarm Clock* is an NDA, and NDAs are usually
Automatically closed when you quit an application. This checkbox, when activated, keeps *Alarm Clock* activated in all your IIGS Desktop applications.

When you're finished setting the options, click the "OK" button. You can select a sound for the alarm and hourly chime if you have the System 6 Sound control panel installed. Just pull up the Sound control panel, select "Attention" from the Event pop-up menu, then select the desired sound from the Sound pop-up menu. (If you don't choose a sound, or if you don't have the Sound control panel installed, you'll get the standard but boring IIGS "bonk.") We suggest a nice bell sound if you have one.

CDEV Alias

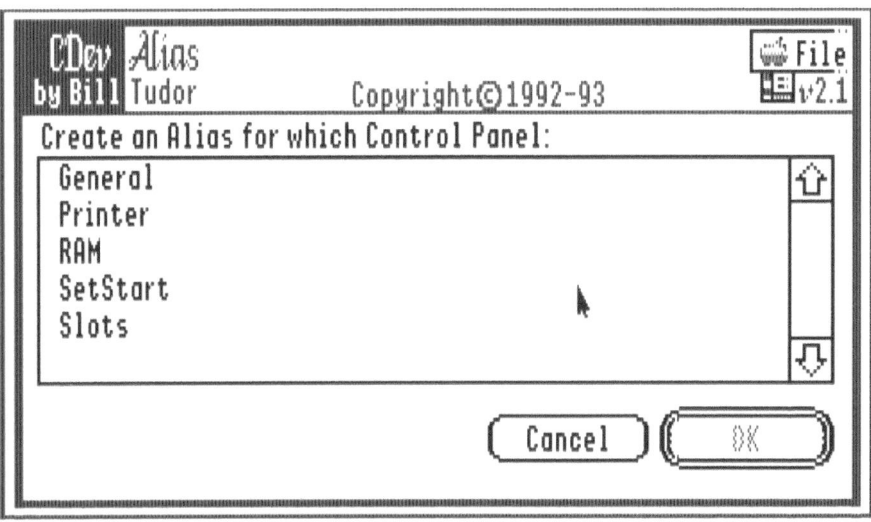

```
CDev Alias                              File
by Bill Tudor      Copyright©1992-93         v2.1
Create an Alias for which Control Panel:
  General                                    ⇧
  Printer
  RAM
  SetStart
  Slots

                        Cancel      OK
```

What It Does

The IIGS Control Panel is pretty simple to use-just open it from the Apple menu, then find the control panel you want to use and double-click it. But if you find yourself using certain control panels a lot, this two-step process can become tedious. The CDEV Alias Finder Extra lets you cut out the middleman and open any frequently-used control panel directly from the Apple menu without first opening the Control Panel itself.

If you use a network, you'll probably want to add the AppleShare and Net Printer control panels to your Apple menu. If you have more than one printer attached to your computer, the DC Printer control panel is a prime candidate. Other frequently-accessed control panels, like Phantasm, Pointless, and Express are also good choices. In short, if you use a certain control panel frequently, adding it to your Apple menu can save you time.

The program's name, *CDEV Alias*, bears a little explanation. A CDEV (see-dev) is a Control Panel Device-or, under System 6, just a control panel – one of those little windows that lets you change one aspect of your system's operation. (The terms "CDEV" and "control panel" are equivalent under System 6.) "Alias" is a Macintosh term which refers to a file that's in two places at the same time, without actually having two copies of the file. *CDEV Alias* lets your CDEVs appear in the Control Panel and the Apple menu at the same time.

Requirements

CDEV Alias requires that the Control Panels NDA be installed and active. You might think that if you add all your Control Panels to the Apple menu, you'd have no need for the Control Panels NDA. Not so! *CDEV Alias* works by asking the Control Panels NDA to open the control panel you created an alias of. If the Control Panels NDA isn't there, it doesn't work – it can't.

We also recommend that you install *IR*. If *IR* is installed, you'll be able to start using your aliases right away. If *IR* isn't installed, you'll have to restart your computer before you see the aliases under the Apple menu.

How to Use It

To add a *CDEV Alias* to your Apple menu, simply select "Create CDEV Alias..." from the Finder's Extras menu. (If "Create CDEV Alias..." isn't on the Finder's Extras menu, make sure it's properly installed, restart, and try again.)

A dialog will appear listing all the CDEVs (control panels) installed in your System folder. CDEVs which already have aliases or which aren't active are excluded from the list.

Just click the CDEV you want to create an alias for, then click the "OK" button. If *IR* is installed, your alias will immediately be added to the Apple menu and that control panel will be opened to confirm your choice. Otherwise, you'll have to restart to see the CDEV under the Apple menu.

To use the alias, just select it from the Apple menu like any New Desk Accessory (NDA). The CDEV will appear on your screen without the intermediate step of opening the Control Panels NDA.

The alias that appears in your Apple menu is actually a small NDA whose only job is to tell the Control Panel NDA to open the control panel. To delete the alias, just open the Desk.Accs folder on your hard drive (inside the System folder) and drag the appropriate NDA to the trash. If you delete an aliased control panel from the CDEVs folder, you'll need to delete the alias from the Desk.Accs folder separately.

Error Messages

If you open a control panel via its alias in the Apple menu, then attempt to open the same control panel again from the Control Panels NDA, without closing the control panel first, you'll get an error message. This error message comes from the Control Panels NDA and is just that program's way of expressing its surprise that the control panel you requested is already open. (It's not used to other programs opening CDEVs behind its back.) The error message is not fatal – just press Return and ignore it.

If you do things the other way (open a control panel with the Control Panels NDA then try to open again it via its alias in the Apple menu) you don't get an error message. Nothing happens.

CPU & Memory Use   5

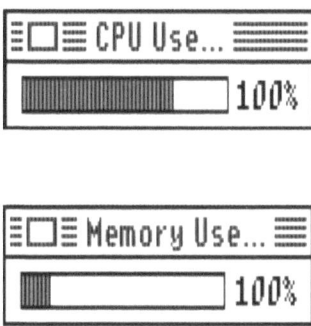

What They Do

CPU Use and *Memory Use* are two simple New Desk Accessories (NDAs) for graphically displaying how much of your system's resources are in use at any time. Both have a small red thermometer, which is updated every half-second or so as long as the NDA is open.

These measurements aren't exact. They're more like the fuel gauge on your car – it doesn't tell you how many gallons of gas you have left, just whether your tank is close to empty. They can help you know when it's time to add an accelerator or more memory.

How to Use Them

Just select "CPU Use" or "Memory Use" from the Apple menu. If you can't find them on your Apple menu, double-check your installation, restart, and try again. A small window with a red "thermometer" bar graph will appear. To close the window, click the small box at the upper left corner of the window, or choose "Close" from the File menu.

CPU Use shows that some of your computer's computing power is being used all the time. It may be mystifying to see that the Finder uses about half the computer's capabilities just sitting there. That's because the Finder is constantly checking your 3.5" drives to see if you've inserted or ejected a disk. You don't usually notice because the Finder stops this activity when you ask it to do something.

CPU Use works by asking the System Software to update the thermometer every half-second, then measuring how much time actually passes between updates. (The busier the system is, the less frequent the updates will be.) Thus, the thermometer doesn't tell you how busy the computer is night this second, it tells you how busy it was in the last second or two. Some actions such as inserting a 3.5" disk may cause the *CPU Use* thermometer to "freeze" for a moment because the computer is busy with another task.

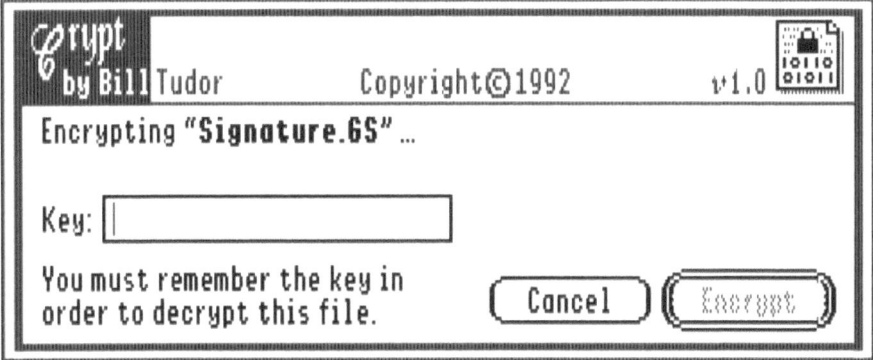

What It Does

Crypt allows you to encrypt document files so the data will become unreadable to anyone but yourself and those who know the key – the "password" – you used to encrypt the file. Naturally, you can later decrypt the file to read it.

Crypt's encryption algorithm is not designed to thwart foreign spies or domestic ones, for that matter. But it's quite effective for providing basic security for your data – it'd take a pretty bright hacker to decrypt a file based solely on an inspection of the encrypted file.

Crypt doesn't encrypt the existing file. Instead, a new file is created containing the encrypted contents of the original file. You can delete the original yourself after creating the encrypted file if you like. Decryption works the same way-the encrypted file is left intact, and a new file is created containing the decrypted data.

If you plan to exchange encrypted files with someone else, the other person will also need a copy of *Crypt*. Please remember that it is a violation of copyright law to simply give a copy of Crypt to another person – they should purchase their own copy of *Six Pack*.

How to Use It

Encrypting a File

Click the file (or files) you want to encrypt. (You can't encrypt folders, though you can encrypt all the individual files in a folder.) Select "Encrypt..." from the Finder's Extras menu. (If you don't see "Encrypt..." on the Extras menu, check your installation, restart, and try again. If "Encrypt..." is there but is dimmed, select one or more document icons and check again.)

The *Encrypt* dialog will appear. Enter a key up to twenty characters long and press Return or click the "Encrypt" button. Now a Standard File Save dialog will appear – name the encrypted version of the file and press Return or click Save. (You may also place the encrypted file in a different folder via the Save dialog.)

If you have selected more than one file, the *Encrypt* dialog will reappear to allow you to specify the key for the next file. (*Crypt* remembers the key you used to encrypt the last file in this batch, making it easy to encrypt a batch of files with the same key. Just press Return to accept the default key in this case.)

Decrypting a File

Decrypting files works just like encrypting them. Click the encrypted file or files and select "Decrypt..." from the Extras menu. (If you don't see "Decrypt..." on the Extras menu, check your installation, restart, and try again. If "Decrypt..." is there but is dimmed, select one or more encrypted files and check again.)

The Decrypt dialog will appear. Enter the key that was used to encrypt the file and press Return or click "Decrypt." If you entered the wrong key, *Crypt* will tell you so. A standard File Save dialog will appear – enter the name for the decrypted file. (You can also place the file in a different folder via the Save dialog.) If you selected more than one encrypted file, the Decrypt dialog will keep reappearing until you've decrypted all the files.

Choosing a Key

Choose a good key which will provide maximum security for your encrypted file. Stringent security will be more of a priority for some people than for others – some of these suggestions may be overkill depending on your situation. There's no reason for a whole cloak-and-dagger routine if you're just protecting your recipe file, but if you're encrypting the source code for a hot new program you've developed, you may want to consider some of these precautions:

- Don't choose an obvious key, like your name, the file's name, your birthdate, your phone number, or your social security number. The key should ideally be something that only you (and other people you give the key to) will know about. It shouldn't be something that can be guessed from public knowledge about you.

- Don't use short words or simple patterns of letters (like "abcd"). The longer the key, the more difficult it will be to crack. Use at least ten characters-fifteen to twenty whenever possible.

- Don't use only letters in your key. Beef up your security with numbers and special characters.

- Don't use completely random keys. True, the most secure keys are totally random strings of characters – gibberish. However, it's virtually impossible to remember them without writing them down. If you write down your key, then you have to take extra precautions to make sure no one has access to it. In most cases a few easily remembered (if nonsensical) English words with a few numbers and symbols thrown in are sufficient.

- Change keys frequently to ensure that even if someone does learn your key, it won't be good for very long.

- If you're exchanging encrypted files with another person, you'll need to agree on a key, and you'll need some way to keep each other informed of changes in the key. The best way to do that is in person. If that's not possible, sending hints like "the key is the name of my favorite band" (which the other person might know is "Tangerine Dream") can be useful.

- The MoreInfo Finder Extra can help enhance your security by making your files invisible and disabling their read access. Use MoreInfo to re-enable their read-access so you can read them. (Anyone can see the files by unchecking "Hide invisible files" in the Finder's Preferences dialog, but they might not even look for something that doesn't appear to be there.)

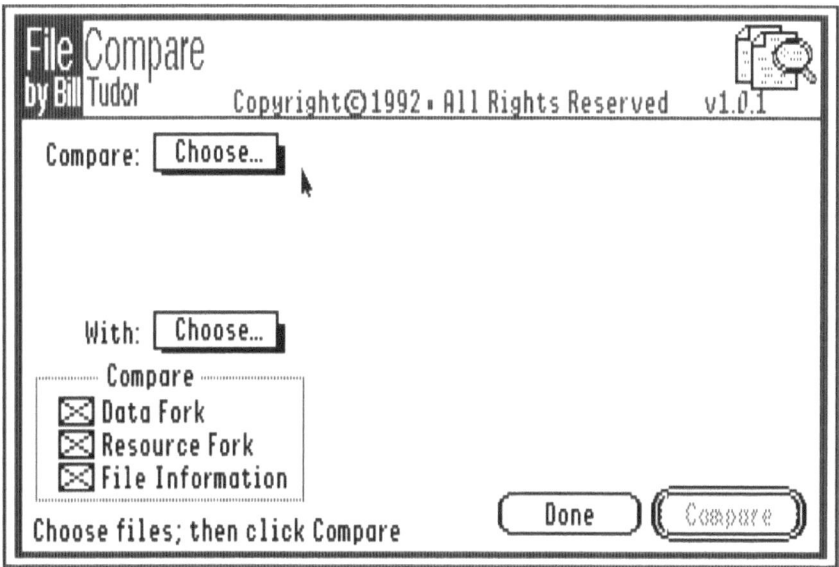

What It Does

File Compare provides a simple way to check for the differences between two files. Use it to find out which of two identically-named files contains the information you need, or to see exactly where those *AppleWorks* patches you applied ended up.

How to Use It

First, select the files you want to compare if they're in the same window. (You can't compare folders, only programs and documents.) If the two files are not in the same window, select one of them-or none at all – there's a way to select files from within *File Compare*. Now select "Compare Files..." from the Finder's Extras menu. (If "Compare Files..." isn't on your Extras menu, check your installation, restart, and try again.) The *File Compare* dialog will appear.

The names of the files you selected should appear next to the words "Compare" and "With." (If you selected one-or no-files, one or both of these items will say "Choose..." Click the word "Choose" and a standard File Open dialog will appear to allow you to select the file.)

Use the checkboxes at the lower right of the dialog to select what parts of the file you want to compare: its file information, its resource fork, and/or its data fork. Then click the "Compare" button.

When *File Compare* detects a difference in the two files, the offending parts of the two files will be displayed in a split-screen hex/ASCII view. The information that differs will be displayed in red. Click "Next" to look for the next difference, or "Done" to move on to the next part of the file (for example, if you're comparing the files' data forks, clicking "Done" will move on to compare the files' resource forks.)

Resource forks are a relatively recent development in the IIGS world. They provide a convenient place for programmers to store data needed by a program without having to use a separate file. Some data files also include a resource fork.

See the "MoreInfo" chapter for more about the file information displayed by *File Compare*.

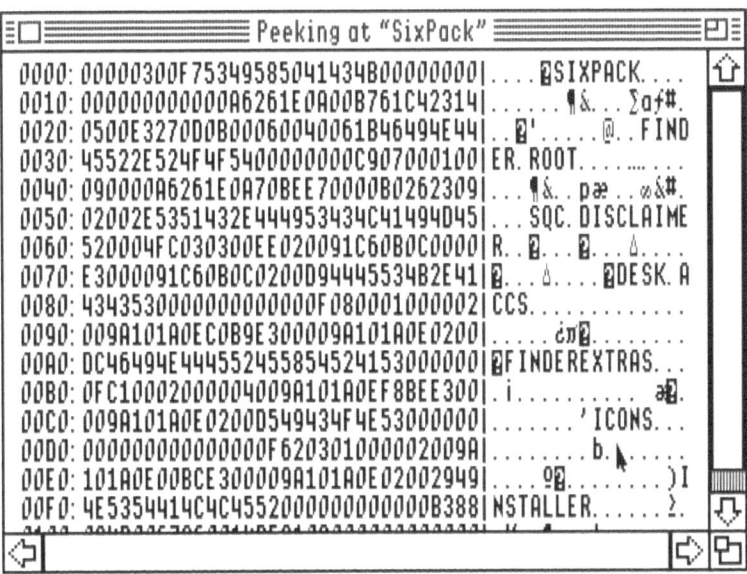

What It Does

FilePeeker gives you a quick way to "peek" at the contents of
virtually any kind of file: text and word processing files, Applesoft
programs, graphics files, icon files, font files, sound files – even
ShrinkIt archives.

FilePeeker is not designed to give you an in-depth, complete
view of the contents of a file. Instead-as its name implies-it lets you
"peek" inside a file to see if it contains the information you think it
does. This can be invaluable, for example, when you have a dozen
graphics files with names like "Image.001."

So when peeking at a word processing file, you'll see the text
of the file, but without the formatting you'd see if you opened the
file in the word processor that created it. (If the file is lengthy you
might not see all of it.) When peeking at a graphics file, you'll see the
picture itself, but it won't have the same colors as it would in the paint
program you drew it in. You should still be able to get a good idea of
what the document is, though.

How to Use It

To peek inside a file, simply click the file's icon or icons – *FilePeeker* can open multiple files at once. Then select "Peek at File" from the Finder's Extras menu. If "Peek at File" isn't on the Extras menu, double-check your installation, restart, and try again.

FilePeeker opens a window for each file's contents – you can open as many windows as you want, up to the limit of available memory. (Sound files are the exception – they're just played, and no window is opened.) The first eight to sixteen kilobytes of the file (depending on the file's type) is displayed. The windows can be moved, resized, and even left open while you work with other windows. *FilePeeker* knows the format of the following kinds of files and displays them appropriately:

Text files (TXT)	Binary II files
Source code (SRC)	NuF'X (ShrinkIt) files
Teach documents	NuF'X in Binary II (Bxy) files
AppleWorks WP	Applesoft BASIC programs
AppleWorks GS WP	Word Search Game Puzzles
File Type Descriptor	Packed IIGS Graphics
IIGS Icon files	Apple Preferred (APF) IIGS Graphics
IIGS Font files	Unpacked IIGS Graphics
WorkSet documents	Sound Resource file (rSound)

If you peek at other types of files, *FilePeeker* displays a hex/ASCII view of the first 256 bytes or so of the file's contents.

You can override *FilePeeker's* default display of files and force it to display a hex/ASCII view of any file by holding down the Option key as you select "Peek at File." You can force *FilePeeker* to display the contents of any file as text by holding down the Shift key as you select "Peek at File."

In addition to the "Peek at File" option, which works with any type of file, *FilePeeker* will automatically peek into icon, font, rSound, and File Type Descriptor files when you double-click them. (If you have set up an application to open these types of files – for example, a sound, icon, or font editor-via a custom icon, *FilePeeker* will not override those links. You can still peek at these files using the "Peek at File" option on the Extras menu.)

26

Hotkeys

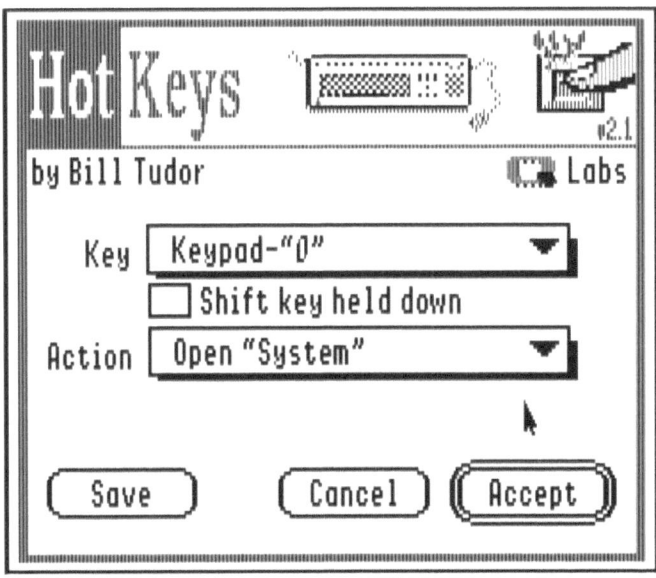

What It Does

Although the Apple IIGS Finder includes keyboard equivalents for many of its menu options, many features don't include keyboard equivalents. *HotKeys* adds these functions to your numeric keypad and, on extended keyboards, to the F-keys at the top of the keyboard. Best of all, you decide which keys perform which functions!

How to Use It

The Pre-defined HotKeys

HotKeys comes with several useful functions already defined. You can start using these keys right away. (All keys are numeric keypad keys, not main keyboard keys.) If these keys don't seem to work, check your installation, restart, and try again.

0	Open System folder on boot disk
1	Open System.Setup folder on boot disk
2	Open Desk.Accs folder on boot disk
3	Open CDevs folder on boot disk
4	Open Icons folder on boot disk
5	Open Fonts folder on boot disk
6	Open Sounds folder on boot disk
7	Set window view to "by Icon"
8	Set window view to "by Small Icon"
9	Set window view to "by Name"
+	Set window view to "by Size"
-	Set window view to "by Date"
*	Stack Windows
/	Close All Windows
=	Open the Finder "About" window
.	Quit the Finder (to previous application)
shift-/	Close rear windows (all but front)
shift-1	Eject 1st 3.5" disk
shift-2	Eject 2nd 3.5" disk

These keys work only when the Finder is "in front." If a desk accessory or some other non-Finder window (such as a *File Peeker* window) is in front, the *HotKeys* key presses may be ignored. Additionally, *HotKeys* is inactive when you're renaming an icon or filling in a dialog.

Redefining HotKeys

To reconfigure *HotKeys* to your preferences, select "HotKeys..." from the Finder's Extras menu. If "HotKeys..." isn't on the Extras menu, check your installation and try again.

The *HotKeys* dialog will appear. Click the mouse to go past the "About" information.

To assign a *HotKeys* action to a particular key, first select the key from the Key pop-up menu. You can select any of the keys on the numeric keypad, plus function keys F5-F12 if you have an extended keyboard. (F1-F4 are usually used for Undo, Cut, Copy, and Paste operations.) You can assign different actions to a key and its shifted equivalent – use the "Shift key held down" checkbox to tell *HotKeys* which variation, shifted or un-shifted, you are defining.

The Finder uses Enter and Shift-Enter as Return-key equivalents when you have an icon selected (to allow you to rename the icons). For this reason, we suggest you leave both Enter and Shift-Enter unassigned.

The Action pop-up menu displays the function currently assigned to the HotKey you selected, or "Not Assigned" if the key is unassigned. Select the desired action (or "Not Assigned") from the Action pop-up menu. This assigns the chosen action to the selected HotKey. Available actions include:

```
Clean Up                   Open System.Setup
Clean Up By Name           Open Trash
Close All Windows          Quit Finder
Close Rear Windows         Restart Computer
Eject 3.5" Disk 1          Shutdown
Eject 3.5" Disk 2          Stack Windows
Finder Preferences         Validate
Launch Application         Verify
Open "About" Window        View by Date
Open CDEVs Folder          View by Icon
Open Clipboard             View by Kind
Open Desk.Accs             View by Name
Open Folder                View by Size
Open Fonts Folder          View by Small Icon
Open Icons Folder
Open Sounds Folder
Open System Folder
```

If you assign "Open Folder" to a HotKey, you'll be presented with a standard File Dialog. Move into the folder you want the HotKey to open and click the "Accept" button. If you assign "Launch Application" to a HotKey, use the standard File Dialog to select the application you want to launch.

Once you've assigned the HotKeys the way you want them, click the "Save" button to save them permanently, or the "Accept" button to use them only until you restart the computer.

Once you have used the "Save" button, the "About" screen you see when you first open HotKeys will go away. You can view it again by clicking the top part of the "HotKeys" dialog.

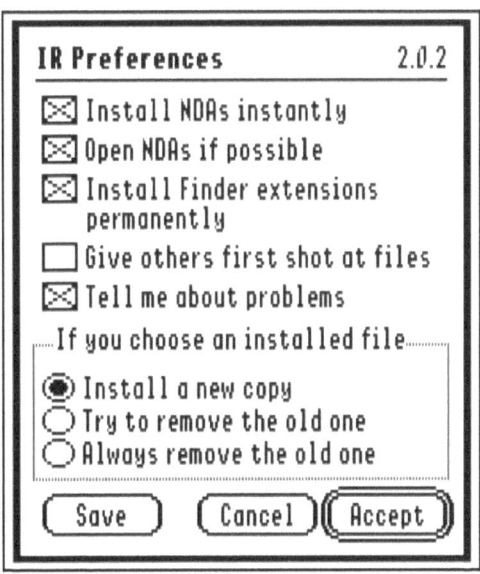

What They Do

IR lets you install Desk Accessories (New and Classic), Finder Extras, inits, and drivers "on the fly." That is, you don't need to keep these items inside your System Folder so they load at startup – you can load them as you need them with the Finder. That way, they don't require any memory until you actually use them.

IR also provides a way for other programs to "call" it and tell it to do things. This allows the *CDEV Alias* program to automatically install the alias it just created, for example.

We've also included a separate New Desk Accessory (NDA) called *OpenSesame*, which allows you to install all the things *IR* can install from within any program, not just the Finder. (Actually, *OpenSesame* works with any Finder Extra which can open things, not just *IR*.)

IR stands for "Init Restarter" because the original version only worked with inits. It's pronounced "ear" like the Spanish verb for "to go."

IR was written by Matt Deatherage and is © 1992 Apple Computer. It was licensed for distribution with *Six Pack*.

How to Use It

Installing System Files with IR

When *IR* is installed, you can install a Desk Accessory, init, Finder Extra, or driver by simply double-clicking it. If this action yields the "Application can't be found" message, *IR* may not be properly installed. Check your installation, restart, and try again.

Having *IR* in your System folder means that you don't have to keep infrequently-used system elements (particularly desk accessories) in your System folder all the time. Lots of desk accessories means less memory for your programs and longer boot times. Even though these DAs don't appear in your Apple menu, you can double-click the NDA's icon in the Finder and they'll open like magic, and appear in your Apple menu until you restart.

The same trick works with drivers. If you rarely use 5.25" disks, you can move your 5.25" driver out of the System folder. Then double-click it whenever you want to use it in a Finder session – voila, your 5.25" drives appear. Even inits like Apple's *GSBug* debugging utility and the *System 6 Special Aids* can be installed with *IR*.

IR Preferences

To change the way *IR* works, select "IR Preferences..." from the Extras menu. (If you can't find "IR Preferences..." on your Extras menu, check the installation, restart, and try again.) You can change these preferences:

Install NDAs Instantly	Tells *IR* to install NDAs in the Apple menu as soon as you double-click them. (If this item is unchecked, the Apple menu isn't updated until you launch another application.)
Open NDAs If Possible	Tells *IR* to automatically open NDAs as soon as they're installed. (If this item is unchecked, the NDA is only installed in the Apple menu.)
Install Finder Extensions Permanently	Tells *IR* to install Finder Extras for the remainder of the session (until you restart). (If this item is unchecked, Finder extensions go away when you leave the Finder.)
Give Others First Shot At Files	Tells *IR* to allow other applications and Finder Extras to try to open the files before *IR* does. (This is designed to allow future extension of *IR* by other programs.)
Tell Me About Problems	Tells *IR* to report problems it encounters while trying to install a system file.
If You Choose An Installed File	Tells *IR* how to handle installation of system files that are already installed. If 'Install a new copy" is selected, *IR* leaves the old version in memory. If "Try to remove the old one" is selected, *IR* will ask the old version to go away before installing the new version. (Some system files won't or can't go away. In that case you'll have two versions in memory.) If "Always remove the old one" is selected, *IR* will refuse to load the new version if the old one can't or won't go away.

Clicking "Accept" uses the preferences until you restart – clicking "Save" saves the preferences to disk for future use as well.

Using the OpenSesame NDA

To use the *OpenSesame* New Desk Accessory (NDA), select
it from the Apple menu from any IIGS Desktop program. (If
OpenSesame isn't on the Apple menu, check your installation, restart,
and try again.) A standard File Open dialog will appear. Select the file
(NDA, CDA, Finder Extra, driver, or init) you want to open and click
"Open" or press Return. The *OpenSesame* NDA works by sending a
message around to all installed Finder Extras asking them if they can
open the file. In this case, since you're opening a system file, *IR* opens
the file. (If you have the *EasyMount* Finder Extra that came with
System 6 installed, you can open server alias files with *OpenSesame*.
If you have *FilePeeker* installed, *OpenSesame* can also peek at font,
icon, file type descriptor, and rSound files.)

For *OpenSesame* to work properly in any program except the
Finder, the Finder Extras it talks to must be installed in the System.
Setup folder inside your System folder. Otherwise the Finder Extras
will go away when you leave the Finder, and they won't be around
to respond to *OpenSesame's* request. *IR* is installed in System.
Setup by default. If you want to use *File Peeker* or *EasyMount* with
OpenSesame, drag them to the System.Setup folder and restart.

MoreInfo   11

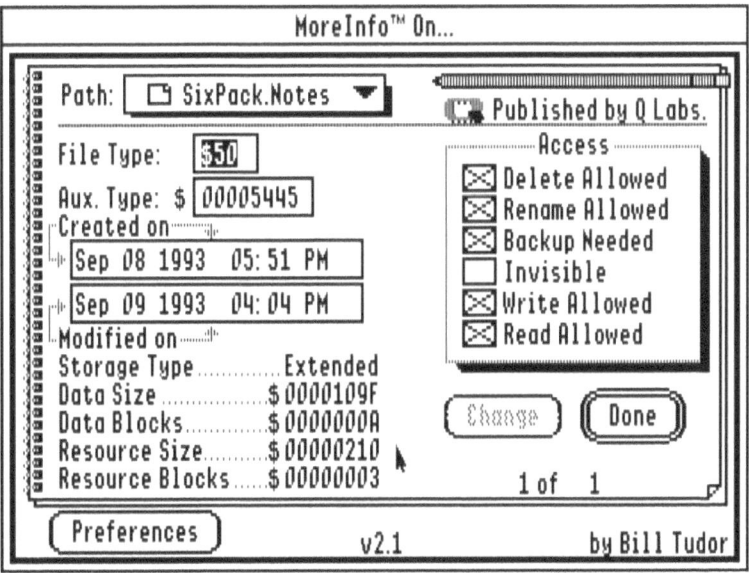

MoreInfo™ On...

Path: 🗂 SixPack.Notes ▼   📱 Published by Q Labs.

File Type: **$50**   ┌─── Access ───┐
                                      ☒ Delete Allowed
Aux. Type: $ 00005445   ☒ Rename Allowed
Created on⌁   ☒ Backup Needed
Sep 08 1993 05:51 PM   ☐ Invisible
Sep 09 1993 04:04 PM   ☒ Write Allowed
                                      ☒ Read Allowed
Modified on⌁
Storage Type............Extended
Data Size...............$0000109F   ⟨ Change ⟩ ⟨ Done ⟩
Data Blocks.............$0000000A
Resource Size.........$00000210
Resource Blocks.....$00000003   1 of 1

⟨ Preferences ⟩   v2.1   by Bill Tudor

What It Does

You're probably familiar with the Finder's "Icon Info" command.
It displays information about the selected icon-its type, its size, its
location, and so on-in a window. MoreInfo enhances the Finder to
allow you to actually change this information. Additionally, *MoreInfo*
provides menu-based shortcuts for common changes you might want
to make to a file's information-to quickly lock or unlock files, or enable
or disable system files.

How To Use It

Getting *MoreInfo*

To activate *MoreInfo*, first select the icon(s) you want info on,
then select "Icon Info" from the Finder's Special menu while holding
down the Shift key, or press ⌘-Shift-I (if you don't hold down the
Shift key, you'll get the Finder's regular Icon Info window.) The

MoreInfo dialog will appear. If it doesn't, check your installation, restart, and try again. The *MoreInfo* dialog contains the following information. It's pretty much the same information you'd get from the regular "Icon Info" command, except it's all on one screen in a slightly different format:

Path   This pop-up menu displays the icon's complete path, starting with the icon's name and listing all the directories it's inside below it. (Choosing an item from this menu accomplishes nothing – it's strictly for informational purposes.)

File Type   A three-letter code representing the file's type as it would appear in BASIC and many other 8-bit programs. (If the type is not recognized by *MoreInfo*, it will be displayed in hexadecimal preceded by a dollar sign.)

Aux. Type   Eight hexadecimal digits showing the file's GS/OS auxiliary type. (ProDOS uses only the last 4 digits.)

For many kinds of files, the auxtype holds important information about the file's contents. For example, a BIN file's auxtype tells BASIC what memory location the file was originally saved from. Some sound files store the sound's playback rate here. For some other types of files, the auxtype is used to divide a general type of file (e.g., graphics) into specific formats (e.g., Apple Preferred). For more information on file types and auxtypes, see "Appendix A."

Created On   The file's creation date and time
Modified On The file's modification date and time

Some programs (such as *AppleWorks*) save files by creating a new temporary file, then deleting the old file. Since the program is essentially creating a new file whenever you save, the file's creation date will only reflect when you last saved it. Other programs overwrite the file's existing data when you save – these programs faithfully maintain the date the file was originally created.

Storage Type The file's GS/OS storage type. On ProDOS disks, storage types can be:

Standard   file has a resource fork
Extended   file has no resource fork
Volume   icon is a volume (disk)
Folder   icon is a folder (subdirectory)

Data Size   The length of the file's data fork in bytes.

Data Blocks   The length of the file's data fork in disk blocks.

Res. Size   The length of the file's resource fork in bytes.

Res. Blocks   The length of the file's resource fork in disk blocks. Resource forks are a relatively recent development in the IIGS world. They provide a convenient place for programmers to store data needed by a program without having to use a separate file. Some data files also include a resource fork.

Access   GS/OS file access flags:

Delete Allowed   file can be deleted
Rename Allowed   file can be renamed
Backup Needed   file has changed since last backup
Invisible   to Finder & most other programs
Write Allowed   file can be written to
Read Allowed   file can be read from

If you selected more than one icon before activating *MoreInfo*, you'll see one or two small green arrows in the lower right comer of the *MoreInfo* window. Click the right-pointing arrow to see info on the next icon in your selection – click the left-pointing arrow to see info on the previous icon. (If you are currently viewing the first file or last icon's info, one of the arrows will be missing.) When you're done viewing info, click the "Done" button.

Changing An Icon's Info

You can modify an icon's Type, Aux. Type, Created on, Modified on, and Access information with *MoreInfo*. Just click the icon and activate *MoreInfo* as usual (hold down Shift while selecting "Icon info" from the Special menu, or press ⌘-Shift-I).

The File Type line-edit field accepts three-letter filetype codes-BAS, BIN, TXT, and so on – as well as hexadecimal codes preceded by a $ symbol ($F1, $00). Changing a file's type only changes what the computer expects to find in the file. It doesn't magically transform one kind of file into another – you can't turn a BASIC program into machine language by changing its type from BAS to BIN, for example. Most of the time you won't need to change a file's type.

The auxiliary type line-edit field accepts eight hexadecimal digits. Remember, ProDOS only stores (and uses) the last four. For many kinds of files, the auxtype holds important information about the file's contents. For example, a BIN file's auxtype tells BASIC what memory location the file was originally saved from. Some sound files store the sound's playback rate here. For some other types of files, the auxtype is used to divide a general type of file (e.g., graphics) into specific formats (e.g., Apple Preferred).

You can change a file's creation or modification date or time with the date and time fields. These fields work just like the Time control panel's date and time fields. Click a part of the date or time, and small arrows appear at the right of the field. Click these arrows to adjust the date or time. Or use the Up and Down arrow keys on the keyboard, or simply type the desired new value. You can also use Tab to move from one part of the date or time to the next.

Access information can be changed by clicking the checkboxes.

When you've made your changes to a file, click the "Change" button. *MoreInfo* will attempt to make your changes, then read the file's info back in and display it so you can see what changes didn't "stick." (For example, you can't change a folder's filetype from DIR, you can't change locked files at all – you can't grant only rename permission to files stored on Macintosh disks because the Macintosh disk format doesn't have such a flag... and so on.)

When you're done with *MoreInfo*, click "Done."

Using *MoreInfo* Shortcuts

MoreInfo adds eight new commands to the Finder's Extras menu for quickly manipulating the information of the selected icon(s). These commands are:

Lock   Locks the selected icons, forbidding renaming, deleting, and writing.

Unlock   Unlocks the selected icons, allowing renaming, deleting, and writing.

Hide   Makes the selected icons invisible to the Finder and most other programs.

Unhide   Makes the selected icons visible to the Finder and most other programs.

To see files you've made invisible (as well as other invisible files used by GS/OS and the Finder), select "Preferences..." from the Finder's Special menu. In the Finder Preferences dialog, uncheck the "Hide invisible files" checkbox, then clock the "Accept" button.

Activate   Makes the selected system files active so they are loaded at startup.

Deactivate   Makes the selected system files inactive so they are not loaded at startup.

Only inits (TIFs and PIFs) Finder Extras, Desk Accessories (NDAs and CDAs), drivers, CDEVs (control panels), FSTs (file system translators), and icon files can be activated or deactivated.

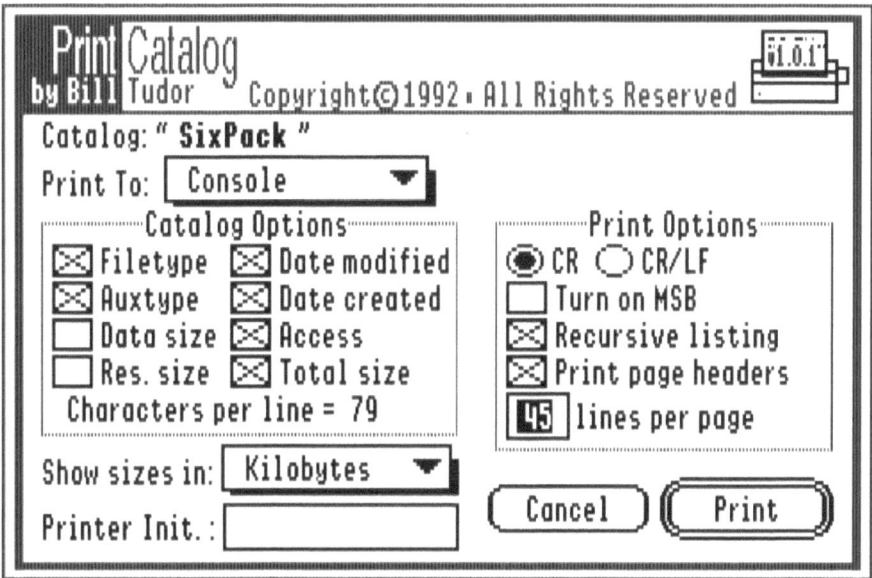

What It Does

Print Catalog is a Finder Extra that prints an "old-fashioned" listing of the contents of a window on your printer (or your screen). Such listings are extremely useful for archival purposes. *Print Catalog* lets you decide what information you'd like to see in the printout.

How to Use It

Open the Print Catalog Dialog

Select "Print Catalog..." from the Extras menu. (If "Print Catalog..." isn't on the Extras menu, make sure it's properly installed, restart, and try again. If it's on the menu but dimmed, bring a Finder directory window-one that contains some files-to the front, and try again. For example, to print a catalog of the contents of a disk called Hard1, bring the "Hard1" window to the front, or open the window if it's not already open.) The *Print Catalog* dialog will appear.

Select a Printer

Below the folder name is a pop-up menu listing the output devices available on your system. On most systems, this menu will contain three items: "Serial Printer," the printer selected in the DC Printer control panel, "Console," the Apple IIGS's text screen, and "Disk File," a file you specify on a disk. (You'll be prompted with a standard File Save dialog for the name of the disk file if you choose "Disk File.") If you have a parallel printer, you'll see "Parallel Printer" instead of "Serial Printer."

If your computer is on a network, you might also see "Network Printer." This printer selection works only if you have already downloaded the ImageWriter emulator to your chosen laser printer using the Net Printer control panel.

Select the Catalog Options

After selecting your printer, check the settings of the Catalog Options. These options let you specify the information you want to see on your printout:

Filetype   Three-letter "old-style" filetype (e.g., BAS, BIN, TXT). If no three-letter code is known, the file's type is displayed as a two-digit hexadecimal code preceded by a $ symbol. For more information on filetypes, see "Appendix A."

Auxtype   GS/OS auxiliary file type. ProDOS files use only the last four digits.

For many kinds of files, the auxtype holds important information about the file's contents. For example, a BIN file's auxtype tells BASIC what memory location the file was originally saved from. Some sound files store the sound's playback rate here. For some other types of files, the auxtype is used to divide a general type of file (e.g., graphics) into specific formats (e.g., Apple Preferred). For more information on auxtypes, see "Appendix A."

Data Size   The size of the file's data fork in blocks or kilobytes

Res. Size   The size of the file's resource fork

Total Size   The total file size (data and resources)

Resource forks are a relatively recent development in the IIGS world. They provide a convenient place for programmers to store data needed by a program without having to use a separate file. Some data files also include a resource fork.

Access   GS/OS access flags in the following format:

D – Destroy-enabled (file can be deleted)
R – Rename-enabled (file can be renamed)
B – Backup needed (file changed since last backup)
I – File is invisible (to most programs)
W – Write-enabled (file can be written to)
R – Read-enabled (file can be read from)

Locking a file by clicking the "locked" checkbox in the file's Icon Info window turns D, R, W access flags off.

Mod. Date   Date the file was last modified

Creation Date   Date the file was created

Some programs (such as *AppleWorks*) save files by creating a new temporary file, then deleting the old file. Since the program is essentially creating a new file whenever you save, the file's creation date will only reflect when you last saved it. Other programs overwrite the file's existing data when you save; these programs faithfully maintain the date the file was originally created.

As you select your catalog options, keep an eye on the "Characters per line" indicator. Standard 10-character-per-inch printouts (the ImageWriter default) are limited to 79 characters. If you select more columns, you need to tell the printer to use compressed print. See the Print Options below.

Select the Print Options

Enter a printer initialization string into the line-edit box at the lower left corner of the dialog box. If you're using an ImageWriter hooked up to a IIGS serial port, you needn't change this string. If you're using another printer or interface card, try the following strings. One of them should work:

`^I80N`   `^I225N`   `^I0N`   `^IN`

The "^" symbol is used to enter control characters (^I in the example above means to send a Control-I character). Check your printer's manual for the codes you need to enter for special features (you can kick an ImageWriter into condensed printing mode with ^Q, for example). Many printer codes contain an Escape character – it can be entered as ^[.

CR or CR/LF   End lines with a carriage return or a carriage return plus a linefeed character. If you get double-spaced lines, make sure this option is set to CR. If everything prints on one line, make sure this option is set to CR/LF.

Turn On MSB   Forces the most significant bit of the characters to be turned on. Leave the MSB turned off when printing to a disk file or to the screen. Leave it turned on when printing to an ImageWriter II. You may need to experiment for other printers.

Recursive List   List the contents of all folders in the window, and all folders in those folders, and so on. Files in folders will be indented one or more spaces as you move "deeper" into a nested folder, producing an easy-to-follow outline.

Page Header   Print a page header on each page. The header includes the page number, the name of the folder being cataloged, and a line labeling the columns that are being printed.

`Lines per Page`	Enter the lines per page here. A normal 8.5" x 11" sheet has 66 lines. To cause *Print Catalog* to leave a margin at the bottom of each page, enter 45 here.
`Sizes`	Print Catalog can report file sizes in either "K" (kilobytes) or disk blocks. Use this pop-up menu to indicate your preference. A disk block is 512 bytes-half a kilobyte. Most people find the "Kilobytes" setting more useful, since that's the way the Finder itself displays all file sizes.

Begin Printing

Once the options are set the way you want, click the "Print" button. If you selected a printer or some other character device, printing will begin. If you selected a disk file, a standard File Save dialog will appear to allow you to name your catalog file and place it in any directory you like.

When printing a catalog to the Console, the IIGS's display will switch to the text screen so you can see the output. Pressing Escape or ⌘-Period will cancel the listing. Press any other key to pause the listing momentarily, then press any other key to resume. Press a key at the end of the listing to return to the Finder.

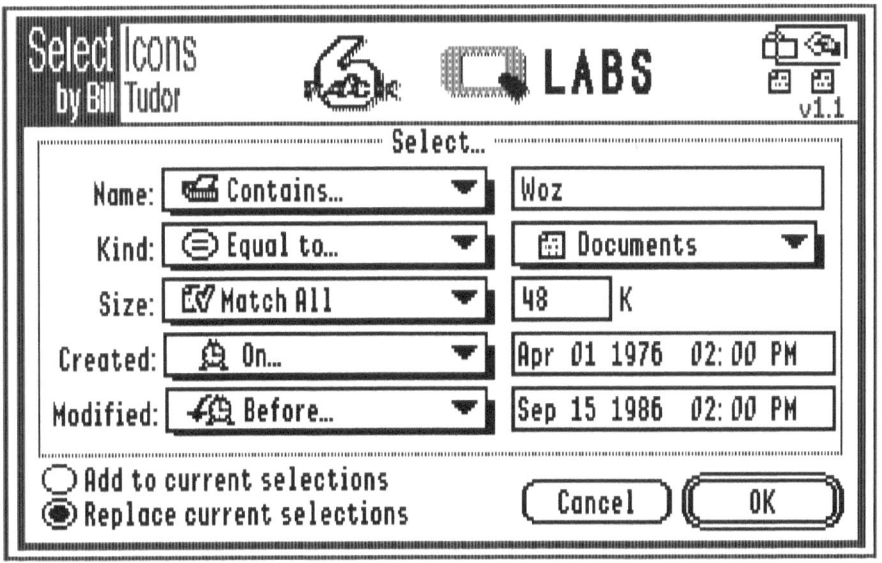

What It Does

Ever wished you could delete all the files that ended in ".SHK" from your disk (to get rid of all those *ShrinkIt* archives you downloaded via modem and unpacked already). Or, move all the documents older than a week or so to a separate folder, and without scrolling through the window and selecting each icon individually?

SelectIcons will help. It lets you select files in the current window by specifying a partial name, a type of file, and a range of creation and modification dates. You can enter multiple criteria and select only the icons that match all your criteria.

SelectIcons can also "memorize" your selection (any group of highlighted icons) and then allow you to re-select exactly the same icons later.

Selecting Icons

Bring a Finder window to the front. *SelectIcons* only works when a Finder window (or the Desktop) containing selectable icons is in front. Choose "Select Icons..." from the Finder's Extras menu. (If "Select Icons..." isn't on your Extras menu, check your installation, restart, and try again. If it's on the menu, but dimmed, bring a Finder window to the front and try again.) The Select dialog will appear.

The Select dialog allows you to specify a number of criteria for selecting files. Each option is selected by a pop-up menu and a field. Each option is restrictive: for example, if you choose "Contains PRO" for the Name field and "Equal to Documents" from the "Kind" menu, you'll select only document icons whose name contains "PRO," not both document icons and other files whose names contain "PRO." (To do that, use the "Add to current selection" radio button. Its use is detailed below.)

When "Match All" is selected for an option, the option is ignored. For example, if you choose "Match All" for Name and enter "Budget" in the Name line-edit field, the name you typed is ignored and icons are selected regardless of their names. Choose an option besides "Match All" from the pop-up menu to cause the Name field to be used as a search option. The pop-up menus are:

Name

`Match All`	Matches icons regardless of name (Ignores contents of Name field).
`Contains`	Matches if icon's name contains specified characters.
`Does Not Contain`	Matches if icon's name does not contain specified characters.
`Equal To`	Matches if icon's name is the same as specified name
`Not Equal To`	Matches if icon's name is not the same as specified name.

Begins With   Matches if icon's name begins with
               specified characters.

Ends With   Matches if icon's name ends with
               specified characters.

Enter a complete or partial file name in the line-edit field to the right of the Name pop-up menu. Letters match regardless of whether they are upper or lower case-"A" matches "a" and vice versa.

Kind

Match All   Matches icons regardless of what kind of file they
               represent (ignores setting of the pop-up menu to
               the right).

Equal To   Matches only icons of the selected kind.

Not Equal To   Matches icons which are not of the selected kind.

Choose the kind of icon (document, application, folder, or system file) you want to select from the pop-up menu to the right of the Kind pop-up menu.

Size

Match All   Matches icons regardless of size
               (ignores contents of "K" field).

Smaller Than   Matches icons smaller than the specified files.

About   Matches icons which are about the specified size
               (within 1K).

Larger Than   Matches icons which are larger than specified size.

Enter a size (in kilobytes) in the "K" field to the right of the Size popup menu.

`Match All`	Matches icons regardless of when they were created or modified.
`Before`	Matches icons created or modified on or before the specified date/time.
`On`	Matches icons created or modified on the specified date (time ignored).
`After`	Matches icons created or modified on or after the specified date/time.

Use the standard date/time fields to select a date and time for the Created and Modified options. (They work just like the date/time fields in the Time control panel.) Click the portion of the date or time you wish to modify, then use the small arrows that pop up at the right of the field to adjust the value. You can also use the up and down arrow keys or simply type a new value. The Tab key moves from one portion of the date/time to the next.

Some programs (such as *AppleWorks*) save files by creating a new temporary file, then deleting the old file. Since the program is essentially creating a new file whenever you save, the file's creation date will only reflect when you last saved it. Other programs overwrite the file's existing data when you save – these programs faithfully maintain the date the file was originally created.

After setting your search criteria, select the appropriate "Add to current selection" or "Replace current selection" radio button at the bottom of the dialog.

"Replace" is the default-if you already have icons selected, *SelectIcons* de-selects them and selects only the ones that match your criteria. If you select "Add," any icons you already have selected remain selected, and *SelectIcons* additionally selects any that match your criteria.

You can use "Add" to select files with multiple criteria at once: to select icons whose names contain either "Junk" or "Garbage," first select all the icons which contain "Junk" (with the "Replace" radio button activated), then select all the icons which contain "Garbage" (with the "Add" radio button selected).

When you're done setting your selection criteria, click "OK" and *SelectIcons* will select all the icons in the front-most window which match your criteria.

Selecting Icons by Filespec

"Filespec" is short for "File Specification." When you choose "Select by Filespec..." from the Finder's Extras menu, a small window appears to allow you to enter a file name. When you press Return, the icon with the name you typed is selected.

You can also select icons by a partial filename using the Filespec window. The "=" sign is a wildcard representing any characters. (You can also use "*" if you prefer – it's equivalent.) It works like this:

PRO=   Selects all files with names beginning with "PRO"
=.SHK   Selects all files with names ending with ".SHK"
=WORK=   Selects all files with names containing "WORK"

The Filespec window can remain open while you use the Finder. Whenever you need to select an icon or a group of icons by name, simply bring the Filespec window to the front, type the comparison information, and press Return.

Saving & Restoring Selections

SelectIcons can also remember which icons are currently selected and re-select them later. The "Save Selections" item on the Extras menu causes *SelectIcons* to make a mental note of the currently selected icons. When you need to select the same icons again later, choose "Restore Selections" from the Extras menu and the icons will be selected again (the window the icons are in is opened or brought to the front if necessary).

The save & restore functions can be useful if you're copying a group of files to a number of different disks. When you insert a new disk, the Finder selects that disk and forgets the icons you so painstakingly selected to copy. So right after you first select the icons you want to copy, just choose "Save Selections." Then, before each copy operation, choose "Restore Selections."

```
┌──────────────────────────────────────────┐
│ ▤☐══════ SuperDataPath™ NDA ═══════       │
│                                            │
│  Application: │ Teach                  │   │
│  Data Directory Path:                      │
│  :SixPack:                                 │
│                                            │
│                                            │
│                                            │
│  ▨ SuperPath™ Active-App. shown above      │
│  ☐ SuperPath™ Active-unlisted Apps.        │
│      ┌───────────┐    ┌───────────┐        │
│      │   Add...   │    │   About   │        │
│      └───────────┘    └───────────┘        │
│      ┌───────────┐    ┌───────────┐        │
│      │  Delete   │    │   Help    │        │
│      └───────────┘    └───────────┘        │
│                                            │
│  ▱📁  v4.1                                 │
└──────────────────────────────────────────┘
```

What It Does

SuperDataPath is a New Desk Accessory (NDA) that provides an easy way to maneuver through your folders from inside the Standard File Open dialog. If you've ever experienced the frustration of trying to remember which folder you put that all-important document in, *SuperDataPath* will help. It provides the following features:

- Allows you to assign a "default" data folder for applications you use frequently – the first time you open a file in that application, you're immediately in that folder.

- Remembers the five folders you used most recently and lets you jump back to them instantly.

- Lets you make a list of other folders you use frequently and jump to any of them instantly.

How to Use It

Linking a Folder to an Application

When a folder is linked to an application, *SuperDataPath* automatically displays that folder's contents the first time you use the application's "Open..." command, instead of leaving you in the application's folder. For example, you could tell *Platinum Paint* to look in your Graphics folder, or tell *ShrinkIt GS* to look in your Downloads folder.

SuperDataPath steps aside once you've opened your first file in a session. The next time you use "Open ... " in the same application, the last folder you used will appear. *SuperDataPath* takes control again when you launch a different application and use its "Open..." option for the first time.

To assign a default folder to an application, first choose the "Open..." command on the application's File menu. Using the standard File Open dialog, move to the folder you want to assign to the application. (The name of the folder should appear at the top of the standard File dialog.) Don't select a file. Instead, click "Cancel."

Now select *SuperDataPath* from the Apple menu. (If *SuperDataPath* isn't on your Apple menu, check your installation, restart, and try again.) Click the "Add" button. Make sure the application name and DataPath displayed in the dialog are the current application's name and the folder you just selected, then click the "OK" button. The folder will be added to *SuperDataPath's* pop-up menu and linked to the application.

To try out the new link, quit the application and re-launch it, then select "Open..." from its file menu. The contents of the folder you assigned should appear, without the need to use the standard File dialog to select the folder. This feature (linking a default folder to an application) is called DataPath. The pop-up menu feature (described below) is called SuperPath. Hence the program's name: *SuperDataPath*.

Removing or Changing a Link

To remove a link, select *SuperDataPath* from the Apple menu. (You don't need to be in the linked application.) Select the application from the Application pop-up menu, then click the "Delete" button.

To change an application's linked folder, first delete the link using the instructions in the previous paragraph, then re-link it following the instructions in the previous section. It is very important to remember to delete the link first before adding a new one.

If you simply add another link without deleting the original link, you'll add a second link between an application and a folder. *SuperDataPath* only uses the first link to determine the application's default folder – the other links merely appear in the SuperPath pop-up menu (see below). We suggest that you maintain only one link for each application and use the technique described in the next section to add folders to the SuperPath pop-up menu to minimize confusion about which folder is the application's default folder.

Using the *SuperDataPath* Pop-Up Menu

SuperDataPath can add a pop-up menu to the Standard Open dialog. This pop-up menu contains the five most recently used folders and all the folders linked to applications using the procedure detailed above. (It can also contain other folders added as described in the next section.)

To enable this feature, first open the *SuperDataPath* NDA from the Apple menu. Select the application to which you'd like to add the *SuperDataPath* popup menu from the Application pop-up menu and make sure the "SuperPath Active – App. shown above" checkbox is checked.

You can also add the *SuperDataPath* Pop-Up menu to applications not linked to a default folder (and thus not listed in the Application menu in the *SuperDataPath* NDA) by checking the "SuperPath Active-Unlisted Apps." checkbox. If this box is unchecked, the pop-up menu will appear only in programs which appear in *SuperDataPath*'s Application menu (and which have their "SuperPath Active-App. shown above" checkbox checked).

To use the *SuperDataPath* pop-up menu, select Open from the File menu as usual. Click the small folder icon in the upper right corner of the standard File Open dialog and hold down the mouse button. Continue holding down the button while you select a folder from the list. (Remember, the list contains all the folders you linked to an application using the FastPath feature, plus the five folders you used most recently.) Release the mouse button after selecting the desired folder. The Open dialog instantly displays that folder's contents.

You'll notice that the pop-up menu displays the complete pathname of each folder. If you're not familiar with pathnames, they're pretty simple. They're a shorthand for the folders you have to open to get to a particular file. For example, if a path was :Q1:Util:ShrinkIt, that would mean that the folder was called "ShrinkIt," and was inside another folder called "Util," which was on the volume "Q1." With a glance, you can distinguish between folders with the same name on different disks or in different folders.

The pop-up menu feature is called SuperPath (the linking feature is called DataPath). Thus the name of the program – *SuperDataPath*.

Adding Other Folders to the *SuperDataPath* Menu

If you want to add other folders to the *SuperDataPath* pop-up folder menu, but not link those folders to any application (for example, if you have graphics categorized into different folders and want quick access to these folders from inside any of your paint programs), that, too, can be accomplished.

Remember in the "Removing or Changing a Link" section we warned you to always change your links by first removing the existing link and then adding a new default folder for that application. We said that this was because additional folders linked to that application would show up in the pop-up menu, but that only the first one would be used for the DataPath feature.

The easiest way to add folders to the *SuperDataPath* pop-up menu without linking them to an application, then, is to link them to a dummy application-an application you never run and which doesn't even have an Open dialog. We've provided just such a dummy application called "None" on the *Six Pack* disk. (It's placed on your hard drive when you install *SuperDataPath*.) We called it "None" so that when you use the Application pop-up menu in the *SuperDataPath* NDA, you see "Application: None." Which, actually, is true – the folder is not linked to a real application. If you try to launch the None application, the Finder will tell you that an error $1104 was encountered. That's because there's nothing in the file. Press Return to return to the Finder.

You can link as many data folders as you like to the "None" program, and all of these folders will appear in the *SuperDataPath* pop-up menu. Here's how to do it:

First, open the *SuperDataPath* NDA from the Apple menu. (It doesn't matter what program you're in when you do this-the Finder is fine.) Then click the "Add" button. Now click the "New" button – don't click "OK." If you click "OK" you'll add a link for the Finder, or whatever program you're in. Probably not what you wanted to do.

After you click "New," a standard File Open dialog will appear to allow you to select an application to link the new folder to. Select the dummy application "None" from the dialog and click "Open." Next, a standard File Save dialog will appear, move inside the folder you want to add to the pop-up menu and click "Accept." (The folder's name should appear at the top of the dialog.) You can also create a new folder if you need to-type the name of the new folder into the line edit field, then click the "New Folder" button, then click "Accept."

Now the proper application and DataPath you just selected should appear in the dialog. Click "OK" to add the path.

Launch an application and try the *SuperDataPath* pop-up menu. You should see the folder you just added. Congratulations!

To delete the folder from the pop-up menu, open the *SuperDataPath* NDA. The Application pop-up menu may contain several "None" entries. Select them one after another until the proper folder path appears under the "Data Directory Path." Then click "Delete."

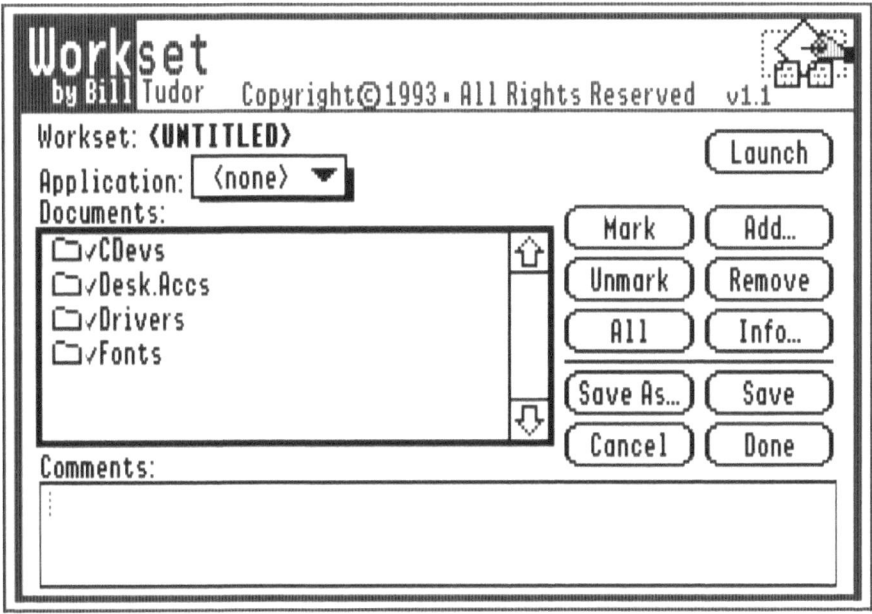

What It Does

Workset is a Finder Extension which allows you to store groups of related files into a single "workset" file, then open all the files in the group at once simply by double-clicking the "workset" file. For example, if you're managing your cash (or lack thereof) using *AppleWorks GS*, you might include your budget spreadsheet, your check register spreadsheet, and a database of all your creditors in a single work set called Budget.Stuff. Then you could double-click Budget.Stuff to launch *AppleWorks GS* and open your three budget files-in one fell swoop.

Most IIGS-specific application programs support opening multiple files in this way. (The ones that don't are obvious-for example, *HyperCard GS* can only open one stack at a time due to the way the program is designed.) *Workset* is also useful for other purposes-including, but not limited to, mimicking the Macintosh's "alias" feature.

How to Use It

Creating a Workset

To create a workset, select "Create Workset..." from the Finder's Extras menu. (If "Create Workset..." isn't on the Extras menu, check your installation, restart, and try again.) The *Workset* dialog appears. (The dialog appears when you edit an existing workset – more later.)

Application   A pop-up menu to select the application which you want to use to open your documents. (If you leave this set to "None," Workset will tell the Finder to open the documents, if the Finder knows which application they "belong to.") Select" Choose..." from this menu to select an application. You can use this feature to open documents in programs other than the one that created them-as long as the program you chose can open the documents in the workset.

Documents   A list of the documents and folders in the workset. You can add a virtually unlimited number of files to the document list. This list also shows which are "marked" with a check mark and which are "unmarked." (Only marked documents are opened when you launch the application.)

Comments   You can enter notes to yourself in this field. Use it for reminders or any other purpose you can imagine.

Launch   This button launches the workset, launching the application specified with the documents you chose (or telling the Finder to open the documents if you didn't specify an application). When creating a new workset, you must save it before you can launch it.

Mark   This button marks the highlighted document. Marked documents and folders are opened when you double-click the workset file or use the "Launch" button.

Unmark	This button unmarks the highlighted document. Unmarked documents and folders are ignored when you double-click the workset or use the "Launch" button. You can also toggle a document's marked/unmarked status by double-clicking it in the Documents list.
Add	This button adds a new document to the workset. A standard File Open dialog appears. You can select multiple files and/or folders from this dialog using Shift-Click and ⌘-Click. New files are automatically marked. It is not necessary for all of the documents in a workset to be in the same folder, or even on the same disk.
Remove	This button removes the highlighted document from the workset. (Usually you'll just want to unmark documents you don't want to use anymore. That way they're still handy in the workset if you want to open them again later.)
All	Selects all documents. Handy for removing, marking, unmarking all documents in one fell swoop.
Info	This button displays information on the highlighted document or folder, including a complete pathname and whether the document is "online" (that is, whether the disk it's on is in a drive).
Save/Save As	These two buttons allow you to save a workset once you've configured it the way you want. "Save As" allows you to save the workset under a different name if you're editing an existing workset. "Save" simply saves the workset under its current name. (If the workset has never been saved, either button will present a Standard File Save dialog to allow you to name the file and place it in any folder you like.)
Done	This button dismisses the *Workset* dialog. If you make changes to the workset but haven't saved them, *Workset* will remind you to save your changes

Cancel   This button dismisses the *Workset* dialog. If you have made changes to the workset but haven't yet saved them, Workset does not ask if you want to save them.

Modifying a Workset

Hold down the Option key while you double-click a workset file to reopen the *Workset* dialog. Add or remove any document files, choose a new application, or mark or unmark document files as necessary. Then click "Save" to save the modified workset. (Alternately, click "Launch" to launch the modified workset without saving it-this way, the changes you make are "one-time-only" changes.)

Workset Ideas

The *Workset* concept is more even more flexible than it may first seem. Here are some ideas to get you started:

• Keep all of your most frequently-used *AppleWorks GS* files (from anywhere on your hard drive) in a single workset. Make them all unmarked (click "All" then "Unmark") and then save the workset. Now, whenever you want to use one or more of these documents, just double-click the Workset file while holding down the Option key. The Workset dialog will appear. Double-click the file(s) you want to open (this marks them), then click the "Launch" button. Because you did not save the workset after marking the files you wanted to use, you'll start with a clean slate the next time you Option-double-click.

• Same as above, except keep all your frequently-used folders in the workset. (Make sure the application is set to "none.") When you mark one or more of them and click "Launch," the Finder will open them for you automatically.

• If you have IR installed, list your unused drivers, DAs, control panels, and Finder extras in a workset. Then use the trick above to install any of them – mark them, then click "Launch" without saving the workset.

- Create a separate workset file for each of your applications (with no documents). Place all the worksets in one folder. Set the view of this folder to "By name" and make the window very narrow-just wide enough to see the names of the workset. Keep this window open all the time and you have a handy program launcher. Just double-click one of the workset files to launch an application.

- If you select an application for a workset (instead of leaving the application set to "none" and letting the Finder decide), and if you select a folder as one of the documents in the workset, that folder will become the application's default folder (much like the default folder *SuperDataPath* allows you to assign). The default folder in the workset will override any default folder you have set up with *SuperDataPath*, but only temporarily. Combine this tip with the trick above and you can create a warkset file which, when Option-double-clicked, allows you to select (mark) the application's default folder before launching it.

- Create a workset with a single application, folder, or document for a simple way to emulate the Macintosh's "alias" capability. Just double-click this file in the Finder and the original– wherever it is – opens automatically. This lets you access the same file from several handy locations.

- Create a workset file with no application and your boot disk's System folder for a document. Drag the workset file out of the window it's in and onto the desktop. Now you have a handy alias of your System folder on the desktop-you don't have to open your boot disk's icon to get to it!

Workset is flexible enough to be helpful in a variety of situations. It can help keep you organized and provide shortcuts for accessing common applications, documents, and folders. You'll probably think of dozens more!

Appendix: ProDOS File Types

Here are the three-letter file types originally defined in Apple's "About Apple II File Type Notes" tech note. In the first alphabetical list, we have weeded out filetypes that you are unlikely to encounter these days on the Apple IIGS. The list afterwards is organized by category.

In many file types, the file's auxiliary type is used to distinguish between one type of document and another. For example, in the LBR file type ($E0), aux type $8002 means that the file is a *Shrinkit* (NuFX) document. Auxtype $800C means that the file is a *Crypt* encrypted file. Both are displayed generically as LBR files in many programs. Graphics, sound, and many other "generic" filetypes are divided similarly.

File types $F1-$F8 are user-definable – any program can use these file types for any purpose. Three-letter file types are used by *MoreInfo* and *PrintCatalog*.

Type   Hex   Description

Type	Hex	Description
8IC	$2C	Apple II Interpreted Code
8LD	$2D	Apple II Language Data
8OB	$2B	Apple II Object Code
8SC	$2A	Apple II Source Code
ADB	$19	*AppleWorks* Database
ANI	$C2	*PaintWorks* animation
ANM	$5B	Animation file
ASP	$1B	*AppleWorks* Spreadsheet
ATK	$E2	AppleTalk data
AWP	$1A	*AppleWorks* Word Processor
BAD	$01	Bad blocks file
BAS	$FC	Applesoft BASIC program
BDF	$AD	Apple IIGS BASIC data
BIN	$06	Binary data or program code
BIO	$6B	PC Transporter BIOS

CDA	$B9	Classic desk accessory
CDV	$C7	Control Panel device
CFG	$5A	Configuration file
CMD	$F0	BASIC command
COM	$59	Communications file
DBM	$D8	*DB Master* document
DIR	$0F	Folder (subdirectory)
DOC	$BF	GS/OS Document
DRW	$53	Drawing
DVR	$BB	GS/OS Device Driver
DVU	$5E	Development Utility
EDU	$56	Educational data
ENT	$5D	Game/entertainment document
EXE	$B5	GS/OS shell application
FND	$C9	Finder data
FON	$C8	Font
FOT	$08	Apple II packed graphics data
FST	$BD	GS/OS File System Translator
FTD	$42	File Type Descriptors
GDB	$52	Apple IIGS Database
GDP	$54	Apple IIGS Desktop Publishing document
GSB	$AB	Apple IIGS BASIC program
GSS	$51	Apple IIGS Spreadsheet
GWP	$50	Apple IIGS Word Processor
HDV	$6F	PC Transporter hard drive volume
HLP	$58	Help file
HMD	$55	Hypermedia document
ICN	$CA	Icons
INS	$D6	Instrument
INT	$FA	Integer BASIC program (also *Beagle Compiler*)
IVR	$FB	Integer BASIC variables (also *Beagle Compiler*)
LBR	$E0	Archival library (*ShrinkIt*, *Crypt*, etc.)
LDF	$BC	Generic load file
LIB	$82	Apple IIGS library file

MDI	$D7	MIDI data
MUM	$5C	Multimedia document
MUS	$D5	Music sequence
NDA	$B8	New Desk Accessory
OBJ	$B1	Apple IIGS object code
OCR	$41	OCR Data
OOG	$C5	Object-oriented graphics
OS	$F9	GS/OS system file
P8C	$2E	ProDOS 8 Code Module
PAL	$C3	*PaintWorks* palette
PAS	$EF	Pascal area
PFS	$16	*PFS* document
PIC	$C1	Super Hi-res picture
PIF	$B6	Permanent initialization file
PNT	$C0	Packed Super Hi-res picture
PRE	$6E	PC Transporter pre-boot
R16	$EE	EDASM 816 relocatable file
REL	$FE	Relocatable code
RTL	$B4	GS/OS run-time library
S16	$B3	GS/OS application
SCR	$C6	Script
SND	$D8	Sampled sound
SRC	$B0	Apple IIGS source code
STN	$57	Stationery
SYS	$FF	ProDOS 8 application or system file
TDF	$AC	Apple IIGS BASIC TDF
TDM	$20	Desktop Manager document
TDR	$6D	PC Transporter driver
TIF	$B7	Temporary initialization file
TOL	$BA	Apple IIGS Tool
TXT	$04	ASCII text
UNK	$00	Unknown filetype
VAR	$FD	Applesoft BASIC variables
WP	$A0	*WordPerfect* document

$0x Types: General

$00   UNK   Unknown

$01   BAD   Bad Block

$02   PCD   Pascal Code

$03   PTX   Pascal Text

$04   TXT   ASCII Text
               Auxiliary type is 0 for a sequential
               text file or the record length for a
               random-access text file.

$05   PDA   Pascal Data

$06   BIN   Binary File or Program Code
               Auxiliary type is binary
               file's loading address.

$07   FNT   Apple III Font

$08   FOT   Hi-Res/Double Hi-Res Graphics

$09   BA3   Apple III BASIC Program

$0A   DA3   Apple III BASIC Data

$0B   WPF   Generic Word Processing

$0C   SOS   SOS System File

$0F   DIR   ProDOS Directory

$1x Types: Productivity

$10   RPD   RPS Data

$11   RPI   RPS Index

$12   AFD   AppleFile Discard

$13   AFM   AppleFile Model

$14   AFR   AppleFile Report

$15   SCL   Screen Library

$16   PFS   PFS Document

$19	ADB	AppleWorks Database
$1A	AWP	AppleWorks Word Processing
$1B	ASP	AppleWorks Spreadsheet

$2x Types: Code

$20	TDM	Desktop Manager File
$21	IPS	Instant Pascal Source
$22	UPV	UCSD Pascal Volume
$29	3SD	SOS Directory
$2A	8SC	Source Code
$2B	8OB	Object Code
$2C	8IC	Interpreted Code
		$8003 – Apex Program File
$2D	8LD	Language Data
$2E	P8C	ProDOS 8 Code Module

$4x Types: Miscellaneous

$41	OCR	Optical Character Recognition
$42	FTD	File Type Definitions

$5x Types: Apple IIGS General

$50	GWP	Apple IIGS Word Processing
		$5445 – Teach
		$8001 – DeluxeWrite
		$8010 – AppleWorks GS
$51	GSS	Apple IIGS Spreadsheet
		$8010 – AppleWorks GS
$52	GDB	Apple IIGS Database
		$8010 – AppleWorks GS
		$8011 – AppleWorks GS Template
		$8013 – GSAS

$53	DRW	Drawing Object Oriented Graphics

$8010 - AppleWorks GS

$54	GDP	Apple IIGs Desktop Publishing

$8002 - GraphicWriter
$8010 - AppleWorks GS

$55	HMD	HyperMedia

$0001 - HyperCard GS
$8001 - Tutor-Tech
$8002 - HyperStudio
$8003 - Nexus

$56	EDU	Educational Program Data

$57	STN	Stationery

$58	HLP	Help File

$59	COM	Communications

$8010 - AppleWorks GS

$5A	CFG	Configuration

$5B	ANM	Animation

$5C	MUM	Multimedia

$5D	ENT	Entertainment / Game

$5E	DVU	Development Utility

$6x Types: PC Transporter

$60	PRE	PC Pre-Boot

$6B	BIO	PC BIOS

$66	NCF	ProDOS File Navigator Command File

$6D	TDR	PC Driver

$6E	PRE	PC Pre-Boot

$6F	HDV	PC Hard Disk Volume

$7x Types: Kreative Software

$70	SN2	Sabine's Notebook 2.0

$71	KMT
$72	DSR
$73	BAN
$74	CG7
$75	TNJ
$76	SA7
$77	KES
$78	JAP
$79	CSL
$7A	TME
$7B	TLB
$7C	MR7

$7D	MLR Mika City
	$005C – Script
	$C7AB – Color Table
	$CDEF – Character Definition

$7E	MMM
$7F	JCP

$8x Types: GEOS

$80	GES	System File
$81	GEA	Desk Accessory
$82	GEO	Application
$83	GED	Document
$84	GEF	Font
$85	GEP	Printer Driver
$86	GEI	Input Driver
$87	GEX	Auxiliary Driver
$89	GEV	Swap File
$8B	GEC	Clock Driver
$8C	GEK	Interface Card Driver
$8D	GEW	Formatting Data

$Ax Types: Apple IIGS BASIC

$A0   WP   WordPerfect

$AB   GSB   Apple IIGS BASIC Program

$AC   TDF   Apple IIGS BASIC TDF

$AD   BDF   Apple IIGS BASIC Data

$Bx Types: Apple IIGS System

$B0   SRC   Apple IIGS Source Code

$B1   OBJ   Apple IIGS Object Code

$B2   LIB   Apple IIGS Library

$B3   S16   Apple IIGS Application Program

$B4   RTL   Apple IIGS Runtime Library

$B5   EXE   Apple IIGS Shell Script Application

$B6   PIF   Apple IIGS Permanent INIT

$B7   TIF   Apple IIGS Temporary INIT

$B8   NDA   Apple IIGS New Desk Accessory

$B9   CDA   Apple IIGS Classic Desk Accessory

$BA   TOL   Apple IIGS Tool

$BB   DVR   Apple IIGS Device Driver

$BC   LDF   Apple IIGS Generic Load File
                $4001 - Nifty List Module
                $4002 - Super Info Module
                $4004 - Twilight Module
                $4083 - Marinetti Link Layer Module

$BD   FST   Apple IIGS File System Translator

$BF   DOC   Apple IIGS Document

$Cx Types: Graphics

$C0   PNT   Apple IIGS Packed Super Hi-Res Picture
       $0001 – Packed Super Hi-Res
       $0002 – Apple Preferred Format
       $0003 – Packed QuickDraw II PICT

$C1   PIC   Apple IIGS Super Hi-Res
       $0001 – QuickDraw PICT
       $0002 – Super Hi-Res 3200

$C2   ANI   PaintWorks Animation
$C3   PAL   PaintWorks Palette

$C5   OOG   Object-Oriented Graphics

$C6   SCR   Script

$C7   CDV   Apple IIGS Control Panel Device

$C8   FON   Apple IIGS Font
       $0000 – QuickDraw Bitmap Font
       $0001 – Pointless TrueType Font

$C9   FND   Apple IIGS Finder Data

$CA   ICN   Apple IIGS Icon File

$Dx Types: Audio

$D5   MUS   Music

$D6   INS   Instrument

$D7   MDI   MIDI

$D8   SND   Apple IIGS Audio
       $0000 – AIFF
       $0001 – AIFF-C
       $0002 – ASIF Instrument
       $0003 – Sound Resource
       $0004 – MIDI Synth Wave
       $8001 – HyperStudio Sound

$DB   DBM   DB Master Document

$Ex Types: Miscellaneous

$E0	LBR	Archival Library
		$0000 – ALU
		$0001 – AppleSingle
		$0002 – AppleDouble Header
		$0003 – AppleDouble Data
		$8000 – Binary II
		$8001 – AppleLink ACU
		$8002 – Shrinkit (NuFX)
		$800C – Crypt
$E2	ATK	AppleTalk Data
		$FFFF – EasyMount Alias
$EE	R16	EDASM 816 Relocatable Code
$EF	PAS	Pascal Area

$Fx Types: System

$F0	CMD	ProDOS Command File
$F1	OVL	User Defined 1
$F2	UD2	User Defined 2
$F3	UD3	User Defined 3
$F4	UD4	User Defined 4
$F5	BAT	User Defined 5
$F6	UD6	User Defined 6
$F7	UD7	User Defined 7
$F8	PRG	User Defined 8
$F9	P16	ProDOS-16 System File
$FA	INT	Integer BASIC Program
		Also Used by *Beagle Compiler*
$FB	IVR	Integer BASIC Variables
		Also Used by *Beagle Compiler*
$FC	BAS	Applesoft BASIC Program
		Auxiliary type is BASIC program's
		loading address, should be $0801.
$FD	VAR	Applesoft BASIC Variables
$FE	REL	EDASM Relocatable Code
$FF	SYS	ProDOS-8 System File

Glossary

ADDRESS – Memory location, usually expressed in hex.

ALGORITHM – A sequence of steps which may be performed by a program or other process, which will produce a given result.

ALPHABETIC CHARACTER – Any one of the letters A through Z (uppercase and lowercase).

ALPHANUMERIC – Consisting of letters, numbers, and other symbols such as punctuation marks and mathematical symbols.

APPLE – (1) The round fleshy fruit of a Rosaceous tree (Pyrus Malus). (2) A brand of personal computer. (3) Apple Computer, Inc. manufacturer of home computers.

APPLESOFT BASIC – A floating-point BASIC interpreter that is included in ROM. It was the successor to Integer BASIC. See *BASIC*.

ARGUMENT – The value on which a function operates.

ARITHMETIC OPERATOR – An operator, such as +, that combines numeric values to produce a numeric result.

ARRAY – Matrix of variable data. This data is accessed by programs to fulfill a need for table style data in an easy to manage format.

ASCII (American Standard Code for Information Interchange) – A character encoding standard that translates uppercase and lowercase letters and symbolic characters into a 7-bit binary representation having the values 0 to 127. The eighth bit, parity and framing bits are not part of this definition.

ASSEMBLER – A program used to translate as assembly language program into the machine language used by a processor.

ASSEMBLY LANGUAGE – A language similar in structure to machine language, but made up of "mnemonics" and "symbols" that are converted to the machine language of a processor by the assembler.

Well-written assembly language programs usually run faster and use less memory than BASIC programs, but they usually take longer to write and longer to test and debug than BASIC programs.

BASE – In number systems, the exponent at which the number system repeats itself; the number of symbols required by that number system.

BASIC (Beginner's All-purpose Symbolic Instruction Code) – A programming language that is designed to be easy to learn and use, and encourage people to use computers for simple problem-solving operations. Originally developed at Dartmouth College.

BINARY – The base 2 number system, composed solely of the numbers 0 and 1.

BINARY FILES – Binary files save machine language programs, binary data (which might be automatically gathered from sensors and generated by analog-to-digital converters), etc. Such material may be of arbitrary length and may include in its body any possible binary combination of bits.

BIT – Abbreviation for "Binary DigIT." Either of the binary digits 0 or 1. See *Byte*.

BLOAD – Binary program load.

BLOCK – Storage methodology used by ProDOS for placing data on a floppy disk. Under ProDOS, a 140K 5.25" floppy disk holds 280 blocks (0~279) of 512 bytes each.

BOOT – The process of starting a computer system ("booting up"). A cold boot is starting the computer after it was off. The operating system (DOS 3.3 or ProDOS) is loaded into memory. A warm boot is a reloading of the operating system without a power-down sequence.

BRANCH – To resume program execution at a new location. GOTO and JMP (jump) are branch instructions.

BRUN – Binary program run. The BRUN command in DOS 3.3 and ProDOS causes a binary program to be loaded into memory and run.

BSAVE – Binary program save. The BSAVE command in DOS 3.3 and ProDOS causes the binary data in some portion of memory to be saved as a disk file.

BUFFER – Large temporary memory storage area.

BUG – A program error, often called "an undocumented feature."

BYTE – The amount of storage required to represent one character. Hexadecimal or Decimal representation of eight binary bits: 0~255 in Decimal, $00~$FF in Hexidecimal. 8 bits = 1 byte. 1,024 bytes = 1K or Kilobyte.

CALL – Executes a machine language subroutine contained within the called memory location and onward. Continues until the program code contains an RTS.

CARRIAGE RETURN – The key used as an end of line or end of input terminator. Also called the RETURN key.

CATALOG – A list of all files stored on a disk, sometimes called a "directory."

CHARACTER – A single byte, letter, digit, or other symbol.

CHIP – Tiny pieces of silicon or germanium containing many integrated circuits that perform specific tasks for a computer.

CODE – (1) A number or symbol used to represent some piece of information in a compact or easily processed form. (2) The statements or instructions that make up a program.

COMPILER – A program which translates a high-level language into the machine code used by a computer.

CONCATENATE – To join together, as in C$ = A$ + B$.

CONDITIONAL BRANCH – A branch that depends on the truth of a condition or the value of an expression.

CONSTANT – A symbol in a program representing a fixed, unchanging value. Compare to "Variable."

CONTROL CHARACTER – A special character created by simultaneously typing the "Control" key and another alpha character. These keys are used in the editor for cursor movement, text formatting, and other specified functions. Control-G can be shown as ^G.

CPU – Central Processing Unit. See *Microprocessor*.

CTRL – The "Control" key.

CURSOR – (1) A marker or symbol that delineates where the next action will take place. (2) A programmer who can't find the reason a program is crashing.

DASH (-) – Command that runs a BASIC, machine, EXEC, or interpreter program in ProDOS only.

DATA – Facts or information used by or in a computer program.

DEBUGGING – The process of detecting and correcting errors in a computer program.

DECIMAL – The base 10 number system, composed of the numbers 0 through 9, inclusive.

DECREMENT – Decrease value in calculated steps.

DEFAULT – Nominal value or condition assigned to a parameter when not otherwise specified by the user.

DELETE – Command that removes a file from its directory.

DELIMITER – Symbol to separate data fields.

DIRECTORY – List of files on diskette or part of a group of files on a hard drive. In ProDOS, each directory has a name rather than the "Slot x, Drive x, Volume x" designation in DOS 3.3.

DISKETTE – A 5.25" or 3.5" disk. Apple II 5.25" floppy disks typically hold 140K, and 3.5" disks typically hold 800K of data.

DOS – Disk Operating System such as DOS 3.3 or ProDOS. The user interface between a computer and the applications program. An OS allows the user to execute programs and perform disk operations.

DUMMY – Data with no significance, "GET A$" is a dummy if used just to halt a program.

EDITOR – Text-editing program that allows text to be entered into a data file and manipulated as desired.

ERROR MESSAGE – Message that notifies the user of an error or problem in the execution of a task or program.

EXECUTE – Perform an action specified by a program or computer operator.

EXPRESSION – A formula in a program describing a calculation to be performed.

FAC – Floating Point Accumulator.

FIELD – Contains data which would not normally subdivide.

FIRMWARE – Those components of a computer system consisting of programs stored permanently in read-only memory. Cards for printers and other devices contain firmware.

FLAG – A data bit used to indicate the state of a device or the result of an operation.

FORMAT – Prepare a blank diskette to receive and store information by dividing its surface into tracks and sectors.

FP (FLOATING POINT) – Floating Point BASIC as included in Applesoft.

HEX – Abbreviation of hexadecimal, the base 16 number system.

HEXADECIMAL – The base 16 number system, composed of the numbers 0 through 9, and A through F. Usually notated with a '$' prefix. Hexadecimal is a useful shorthand for describing the contents of a byte, with each hex digit describing half of a byte.

HEX DUMP – Formatted listing of hex data.

HIGH ORDER – The byte containing the value of the left most two digits of a hex expression.

HI-RES – High-Resolution graphics.

INCREMENT – Increase value in calculated steps.

INITIALIZE – (1) To set to an initial state or value in preparation for some computation.
(2) To prepare a blank disk to receive information by dividing its surface into tracks and sectors.

INPUT – (1) Information transferred into a computer from an external source, such as a keyboard, disk drive, or modem. (2) The act or process of transferring such information.

INTEGER – Number without fractional parts in the range -32768 to +32767.

INTEGER BASIC – The BASIC interpreter for the first Apple II. Succeeded by Applesoft BASIC.

INTERPRETER – A program which translates instructions written in a high level to machine code as the program is executed.

INTERRUPT – (1) To temporarily stop a process. (2) A signal created by either hardware or software to demand the immediate attention of a machine's CPU, there by stopping execution of any code that is being executed by said CPU. (3) In data communications, to take an action at a receiving computer that causes the ending computer to end a transmission.

I/O (Input/Output) – The transfer of information in and out of a computer. Used frequently in connection with peripheral devices.

IRQ – Interrupt requests.

JUMP – Another term for a branch.

KILOBYTE (K or KB) – Used with numbers to denote "kilo" or one thousand. 1K = 1,024 bytes. 64K is 64 times 1,024 bytes, or 65,536 bytes.

LABEL – Symbolic name for an address, often expressed in mnemonic form.

LINEFEED – Moves the cursor on the screen down one line. The ASCII character is Control-J.

LOAD – Command that brings a BASIC program into memory from a file.

LOADER – Program that calls up machine code from mass storage and loads it into memory for execution.

LOCK – Command that protects a file from being accidentally renamed, deleted, or altered.

LOGICAL OPERATOR – An operator, such as AND, that combines logical values to produce a logical result.

LOOP – Section of a program that is executed repeatedly until some condition is met such as an index variable reaching a specified ending value.

LOW ORDER – The byte containing the value of the right most two digits of a hex expression.

LO-RES – Low-Resolution graphics.

L.S.B. – The Less Significant Byte of the two-byte pair.

LSB – Least Significant Bit.

MACHINE LANGUAGE – Data groups which are interpreted as instructions to be executed by the processor. See *Assembly Language.*

MEMORY – See *RAM (Random Access Memory)*.

MEMORY LOCATION – A unit of main memory that is identified by an address and can hold a single item of information of a fixed size. In the Apple II, a memory location holds one byte, or 8 bits of information.

MICROPROCESSOR – A computer processor contained in a single integrated circuit, such as the Apple II's 6502 or 65C02 microprocessor.

MNEMONIC – Symbolic abbreviation containing characters helpful in remember an application or function, such as an assembly language instruction.

MOD – Algorithm which returns the remainder of a division operation (must be simulated in Applesoft BASIC).

MONITOR – (1) A closed-circuit television receiver. (2) A program which allows you to use your computer at a very low level, often with the values and addresses of individual memory locations. Monitor commands are used to communicate with the Monitor.

M.S.B. – The More Significant Byte of the two-byte pair.

MSB – Most Significant Bit.

NIBBLE (or Nybble) – (1) A 4-bit unit of data, or half a byte. (2) One of the best and longest-running magazines for the Apple II and Mac, created by entrepreneur and business expert Mike Harvey. (3) "What are we going to call this series of bits? How about a bite, but spell it with a 'y'! So what do we call half a byte? A 'nybble', obviously!" (attributed to Werner Buchholz at IBM, circa 1956.)

NULL – Having no value.

OBJECT PROGRAM – The program produced by a compiler or interpreter from a high-level program.

OFFSET – Value, often used with or as an index to locate related data and add to a base value.

OPERATOR – A symbol or sequence of characters such as + or AND, specifying an operation to be performed on one or more values (the operands) to produce a result.

OUTPUT – (1) Information transferred from a computer to some external destination, such as the display screen, a disk drive, a printer, or a modem. (2) The act or process of transferring such information.

PAGE – Each page of memory in Apple II computers consist of 256 bytes. That is to say, $00 to $FF would be one page. A 32K machine would have 128 pages, a 48K machine would have 192 pages, while a 64K machine would contain 256 pages of memory. After the Zero Page ($0000~$00FF), each page is described by the first two digits of its 4 digit hexadecimal address.

PARALLEL – A method of data handling in which all the bits composing a word are transmitted simultaneously.

PARSER – Section of interpreter that formats listing of a BASIC program.

PATH – A specified route to a specific subdirectory used in ProDOS.

PC – Program Counter.

PEEK – BASIC command which returns the decimal value of a specified memory location.

PERIPHERAL – An external device connected to a computer such as a printer, modem, monitor, or disk drive.

POINTER – A register memory location containing the memory address of data or instructions.

POKE – BASIC command which stores a decimal value in a specified memory location.

PR# – Command that sends output to the Apple II slot number specified.

PREFIX – A settable pathname that indicates a directory file.

PROCESSOR – A generic term for that part of computer hardware performing arithmetic and logical operations. See *Microprocessor*.

ProDOS – The major operating system for Apple II computers, that stands for Professional Disk Operating System.

PROGRAM – A sequence of instructions to be followed by the computer to carry out desired operations.

PROMPT – To remind or signal the user that some action is expected, typically by displaying a distinctive symbol, a reminder message, or a menu of choices on the display screen.

Q LABS – A division of Quality Computers that produced all of the software sold by the company including this wonderful package. See *Quality Computers*.

Quality Computers – A St. Clair Shores, Michigan company from the 1980s and 1990s that provided many useful tools and utilities for the Apple IIGS. Quality Computers president Joe Gleason has given A.P.P.L.E. permission to make these classic programs available again.

QUIT – Exiting a program and returning to the operating system.

RAM (Random Access Memory) – The volatile, temporary storage area in the computer that requires power to maintain its contents.

RAM DRIVE – The use of RAM to emulate a disk drive for temporary drive storage.

READ – To transfer information into the computer's memory from a source external to the computer (such as a disk drive or modem), or into the computers processor from a source external to the processor (such as a keyboard or main memory).

REGISTER – Single RAM memory or microprocessor storage location, usually for temporary use. A, X, Y-Registers and S, P, PC-Registers.

RELATIONAL OPERATOR – An operator, such as >, that compares numeric values to produce a logical result.

RENAME – Change the name of the file.

RESET – A key, which is part of a combination that causes the computer to re-boot a program. To Stop and warm start the computer.

ROM (Read Only Memory) – A memory device from where operating instructions and other programs reside permanently and cannot be altered or added to.

ROUTINE – A program which performs a specified task or function.

RS-232 – A standard voltage interface allowing a serial connection between the computer's communications port and an external device such as a modem or a printer.

RUN – The command to execute a BASIC program.

RWTS – Read-Write Track-Sector. These are the Diskette input and output routines.

SAVE – Command to save the BASIC program currently in memory to a file on disk.

SECTOR – The tracks on Apple 5.25" diskettes are subdivided into sectors. The sector is the smallest unit of information that can be written to, or read from, a diskette at one time. Each sector contains one memory page (256 bytes) of usable information. Each track contains the same number of sectors, so the physical length inches or centimeters of a sector on the outermost track is longer than that of a sector on the innermost track. Sectors on the outermost track and the innermost track take the same amount of time to pass by the read head.

SERIAL – A method of data handling in which the bits composing a word are transmitted one after the other.

STACK – A section of memory used to hold addresses or data items. The page of 256 memory locations from $0100 to $01FF (decimal 256~511) is called the Apple System Stack, as well as memory Page 1. The Stack is used in conjunction with the S-Register or Stack Pointer to provide positive control of the system in situations where control is passed from one portion of a program to another.

STATEMENT – An instruction line in a high-level language. In BASIC, smallest portion of a program complete in itself. Delimited by a ':' or end of line.

STRING – A group of ASCII characters that are alpha, numeric, punctuation, or control.

SUBROUTINE – A section of frequently used operations in a program which are treated as small separate programs.

SYNTAX – The formal structure of an argument or command.

SYNTAX ERROR – An error which specifies to the user that the structure of the line of BASIC code is improperly formatted or that it is missing a required element such as quotation marks.

TABLE – List of values, words, data, etc. that may be referenced by a program.

TEXT FILE – A file containing an arbitrary string of ASCII characters interspersed with occasional carriage returns to specify the end of a line.

TOKEN – One byte hex representation of a BASIC or other high level language command.

TRACE – A debugging method in which the program is executed one instruction at a time, and sometimes the register contents can be examined after each step.

TRACK – Apple 5.25" diskettes have 35 tracks under DOS 3.3. Each consists of a circular recording path at a fixed distance from the center of the disk. Thus, each is like a very thin, at ring, concentric with all the others. They are numbered from 0 (the outermost track) to 34 (the innermost track).

VAL – Applesoft command that solves the value of a string. Also, the founder of A.P.P.L.E.

VARIABLE – Alphanumeric representation which may assume or be assigned a number of values.

VECTOR – Address to be branched to.

VOLUME – In DOS 3.3 and ProDOS, volume refers to floppy disk and hard drive storage.

VTOC (Volume Table of Contents) – On a 5.25" diskette Sector 0 of Track 17 (the track which is equidistant from the innermost and outermost tracks) is reserved for the VTOC.

WHY – Questions that programmers ask that have no answer.

WINDOW – Portion of screen display blocked off for special use.

WOZ – Steve Wozniak, an Apple Computer Inc. co-founder, inventor of the Apple-1 and Apple II computers, all-around genius, nice guy, über geek, philanthropist, and longtime supporter of the A.P.P.L.E. user group.

WRITE – To transfer information from the computer to a destination external to the computer (such as a disk drive or modem) or from the computers processor (such as main memory).

WWA – *What's Where in the Apple: Enhanced Edition* – a very useful programming reference book, also published by A.P.P.L.E.